What people are saying about …

unplanned grace

"*Unplanned Grace* is my new favorite book on helping people understand why every life is sacred. There are accidental parents, but there are no accidental children! Your parents may not have planned you, but God did—and he had a purpose for your birth. This book is biblical, practical, loving, and warmhearted."

Rick Warren, DMin, author of
The Purpose Driven Life

"*Unplanned Grace* fills the reader with hope and healing as it uncovers the personal side of abortion: the scariness of an unplanned pregnancy—often amid abuse—and the unbearable cultural and family pressure that women feel to choose abortion. Individuals and churches will discover dozens of practical tools to help those with unplanned pregnancies."

Jeff Myers, PhD, president of Summit Ministries

"Between the stirring stories and straight-forward statistics, *Unplanned Grace* is a compelling tapestry of grace, showing the pregnancy-help community stepping up to love people facing difficult decisions. This book reveals the bigger picture of the Spirit of God at work with empowering grace."

Jor-El Godsey, president of
Heartbeat International

"*Unplanned Grace* exemplifies what it truly looks like to lead with love and compassion. It's not just about being pro-life; it's about being ABUNDANT pro-life. If you're someone who's pro-life but not sure how to get plugged in, this is definitely the book for you."

Ashley Bratcher, actress (*Unplanned*),
producer, inspirational speaker

"Pro-life advocates are often wrongly accused of caring for the baby only until he or she is born. This book demonstrates through story how pro-life men and women across the country care about the whole person—the moms, the dads, and the babies—throughout the pregnancy and after."

John Stonestreet, president of the Chuck
Colson Center, cohost of *Breakpoint* radio; **Sarah
Stonestreet,** cohost of the *Strong Women* podcast

"*Unplanned Grace* will help Christians more thoughtfully engage the pro-life conversation in society today. It helped me not only empathize with the complexities women (and men) face during unplanned pregnancy but also grow more confident in the creative ways the church can show up in the lives of those affected."

Rebekah Lyons, bestselling author
of *Rhythms of Renewal*

"*Unplanned Grace* is a beautifully written practical guide to understanding the crisis facing parents with an unplanned pregnancy, how pregnancy centers support women's health, and the powerful impact we must have on protecting the most vulnerable."

Karysse J Trandem, DO, OB-GYN,
CEO of Canopy Global Foundation

Foreword by Lauren Green McAfee

Brittany Smith & Natasha Smith

un planned grace

a compassionate conversation on life & choice

DAVID C COOK

transforming lives together

UNPLANNED GRACE
Published by David C Cook
4050 Lee Vance Drive
Colorado Springs, CO 80918 U.S.A.

Integrity Music Limited, a Division of David C Cook
Brighton, East Sussex BN1 2RE, England

The graphic circle C logo is a registered trademark of David C Cook.

The website addresses recommended throughout this book are offered as a
resource to you. These websites are not intended in any way to be or imply an
endorsement on the part of David C Cook, nor do we vouch for their content.

All stories are based on real clients, though some names and
details have been changed to honor the confidentiality and
protect the identities of the persons involved.

All Scripture quotations are taken from the Holy Bible, New International
Version®, NIV®. Copyright © 1973, 2011 by Biblica, Inc.™ Used by permission
of Zondervan. All rights reserved worldwide. www.zondervan.com. The
"NIV" and "New International Version" are trademarks registered in
the United States Patent and Trademark Office by Biblica, Inc.™

Library of Congress Control Number 2021932640
ISBN 978-0-8307-8211-6
eISBN 978-0-8307-8212-3

© 2021 Save the Storks

The Team: Michael Covington, Stephanie Bennett, Judy Gillispie,
Leigh Davidson, James Hershberger, Katie Long, Susan Murdock
Cover Design: James Hershberger

Printed in the United States of America
First Edition 2021

1 2 3 4 5 6 7 8 9 10

061621

Dedication

*To all women and men who face the
unplanned, who experience struggle and fear.
May you find hope, healing, and life. To those
who heroically choose life and to those who
bravely seek healing from past choices …*

*To all pregnancy resource centers and pro-life
organizations that exist to support, educate, and
empower those facing an unplanned pregnancy. To
the health care professionals who volunteer their
time to ensure that more women have access to free
pregnancy care in the hope they will choose life …*

*To the church and the people of God, who are
called to love and care for those who are vulnerable
including moms, dads, and babies. May this book
serve as a catalyst for even more empowered change
and lifesaving choices in and through your church.*

Contents

Section 1: Circumstantial Difficulties

Section 2: Relational Pressure

Section 3: Holistic Health

Section 4: Taking Action

Foreword

Chances are, if you've picked up this book, you consider yourself pro-life and you proudly champion human dignity for all life. But if you've picked up this book and do *not* consider yourself pro-life, chances are you too would champion the idea that every person has dignity and value. People on both sides of the pro-life/pro-choice issue care about lives; where we disagree is in the details.

Real-life examples of the complex decisions required in tough situations can often bring us closer together. Through personal stories, we can connect. This book is significant because it moves beyond tweets and sound bites into actual stories of women seeking pregnancy services. It gets beyond the echo chambers of talking points and highlights the very "rubber meets the road" realities that women and men face.

On a chilly night in November 2012, I had a "rubber meets the road" moment of my own, and being pro-life was going to cost me something. Growing up in the Midwest, I was surrounded by people with similar values, which included the pro-life cause. People in the church cared about the sanctity of life, and as a young person I never heard anyone talk personally about abortion. I knew I considered myself pro-life, but I had never truly grappled with that belief.

In my twenties, I suddenly found my beliefs being tested, but not in the way most people might think. The cost came when a government mandate began to force my family's privately held company, Hobby Lobby, to pay for abortive drugs and devices. If our family did not comply, the fines would be steep and unsustainable for the business. My entire career and livelihood were wrapped up in the family business. The options came down to (1) comply with the government mandate to pay for abortive drugs that went against our convictions about life or (2) resist and face crippling fines that would likely shutter the business.

It was a shift in my experience as a pro-life advocate—my convictions were going to cost me something. If nothing else, they were going to cost my comfort. Was I willing to pay?

I decided I was. In the end, the company's case went all the way to the Supreme Court of the United States, where the court ruled in Hobby Lobby's favor.

I knew that every life is a life and that all life must be valued and protected. But I also learned the importance of knowing you're not alone when facing difficult choices. While my story is different from many people's experience with their convictions about life, the common thread always comes down to the same questions: *What do I truly believe about life in the womb, and am I ready to sacrifice because of that conviction?*

This book beautifully shares stories of real experiences, laments pain and losses, and inspires with ways to practically support life right where you are. Many of the stories brought tears to my eyes—tears of empathy for the very real difficulties that many women and men face and tears of gratitude for the ways people have stepped in and served those in need. This authentic, fresh perspective on the issue of life is needed. Regardless of where you stand on the issue, I urge you to consider these stories.

Lauren Green McAfee
speaker, writer, and Hobby Lobby corporate ambassador

Preface

In 2017, I (Natasha) began visiting pregnancy centers across the country that were connected with Save the Storks, a pro-life nonprofit existing to support pregnancy centers nationally. As I met with staff and toured their clinics, I began to see how holistic and woman-focused pro-life ministries truly are. I recognized the possibility of bridging the chasm between pro-life and pro-choice debates by showing how both ideological systems can agree that a woman's life and well-being are vitally important.

In the years since 2017, I have read countless stories and conducted interviews with individuals who either work in the pro-life world or were empowered to choose life by a pro-life organization. Common themes wove through the stories of hundreds of women who contemplated abortion: "I thought I had no other choice," "I was alone," and "I felt so afraid, I didn't know what I was going to do." But other themes emerged too in the face of hard decisions: hope, joy, education, and true empowerment through compassionate people who readily loved and supported women throughout their journeys.

Hosea 4:6 frequently came to mind and sparked the idea for this book: "My people are destroyed for lack of knowledge." So many pro-life individuals don't understand what makes an unplanned pregnancy difficult or the fear factors that can validate a woman's choice to abort. Likewise, few women know about the many resources that could empower them to choose life. These real stories can both inform the church about the need for pro-life expression and offer tangible ways to love our neighbors well through unplanned grace.

Acknowledgments

Gratitude is the word that comes to mind when we think of those who helped us complete this book. First, we must thank the Lord for His faithfulness in giving us the time, energy, direction, and inspiration to write. We also recognize the power of prayer—and God's answers—and must thank our friends and family who supported us in this way.

This book would have been impossible without the contributions of the pregnancy resource centers (PRCs) across the country that shared their stories with us. Boundless gratitude goes to all those who willingly interviewed with us both at PRCs and at the organizations we featured within this book. It was an honor to talk with such incredible pro-life heroes across the country, and we are deeply appreciative of their passion, ministry, and love for life.

This book would not exist without the incredible foundation of support for women laid by Heartbeat International, Care Net, Embrace Grace, Human Coalition, and so many others.

Our appreciation also extends to the staff and leadership at Save the Storks who made this project feasible, especially Thomas Kim and Diane Ferraro. They established the relationship with our publisher and gave us the time and resources we needed to complete this book. Additionally, we want to give special thanks to Joseph Schmidt and Shara Pierce, who provided valuable editing, feedback, and support.

Matt Hammitt and Mikaela Herndon supported this work from the beginning. Their skillful and creative storytelling brought such depth to the narratives, and we are grateful for their editing contributions.

And finally, a huge, heartfelt thank-you to our publisher, David C Cook, who saw the value of this work and gave us the opportunity to work with Stephanie Bennett, our editor. Her helpful feedback and encouragement throughout the process have been invaluable. Her belief in this work always gave us fresh wind in our sails.

Introduction

Saved by a Text

As Jade left, the door closed slowly behind her, reflecting the hesitation in her mind.

Should she turn back, rush inside the clinic, and just do it? Sitting in her parked car, Jade closed her eyes and took a breath to calm her rapidly beating heart. Consumed by uncertainty, doubt, and fear, Jade was awakened from her numbing trance by a text notification.

> *Hey Jade! It's Liz. I hope you're well. Missed seeing you yesterday for your pregnancy appointment. I'm here for you if you want to talk.*

Jade's heart skipped a beat, and she caught her breath with hope as she reread the message.

She immediately typed back: "Are you open? Can I come over now?"

Without waiting for a reply, Jade threw her car into gear and drove out of the abortion clinic's parking lot to the Arkansas Pregnancy Resource Center located nearby.

"Is Liz here?" Jade asked as she approached the receptionist. "I just got out of my appointment at the abortion clinic. I'm having a difficult time deciding what to do."

"Come on in!" Liz opened the door to the counseling room with a warm smile. What a contrast to the abortion clinic; this room was fresh, cozy, and comfortable. Jade instantly felt a sense of sincere care from Liz as she asked more about her story.

Jade had originally made an appointment at the pregnancy center, but her boyfriend insisted on the abortion clinic. Their relationship was already pretty rocky, and now he was pressuring Jade to have an abortion. She just didn't feel like she could do it again.

"I've had two abortions already," Jade confessed as she examined the floorboards, unable to meet Liz's eyes.

Tears began to blur her gaze, but she blinked them away before her eyes filled.

"It tore me up and I'm still suffering from regret. Honestly, I've been heartbroken."

Losing her composure, Jade bent over, holding her head in her hands. Letting out a deep sob, she blurted, "My heart is so torn."

Liz gave her a tissue and placed a hand on her shoulder. "I'm here for you. You don't have to rush into your decision right now."

After a few minutes Jade continued, "I've been depressed ever since my first abortion, but I felt like it was my only choice at the time. It was the best thing for me—at least that's what I keep telling myself. But then when I had my second abortion, I just felt worse, and I've struggled with the guilt and regret of that decision ever since. Now that I'm pregnant again, I don't feel like I can go through it all a third time. But my boyfriend—he doesn't want the baby."

Understanding the burden on Jade's shoulders, Liz moved the conversation toward a hopeful topic.

"Would you like to have an ultrasound so we can see how far along you are?"

"Yes!" Jade said with a note of excitement. "The abortion clinic did one, but they wouldn't let me see the screen. They didn't give me any information about the fetus. They just said we needed to schedule the abortion soon. I'd really like to see what it looks like."

A few minutes later, Jade's eyes lit up in wonder as she saw a tiny form on the screen. The eight-week-old baby had a strong heartbeat; those little flashes meant the world to her.

When Jade had decided to go to the pregnancy center, she'd called her boyfriend, Wyatt, and asked him to meet her there. *Maybe, if he sees his child, he'll change his mind and want to keep this baby too*, Jade thought hopefully.

Liz immediately noticed a change in Jade when Wyatt entered the exam room. She became quiet, dejected, and passive. They exchanged a few words, but he hardly even looked at the ultrasound screen and was unmoved. He'd made up his mind: abortion was the obvious choice.

After he left, Liz offered Jade additional information about gestational development and local resources, including the pregnancy center's wealth of free materials and classes if she decided to keep her baby.

"Also, I know you've already been dealing with a lot of pain from your past abortions," Liz said. "I want you to know that we have a after-abortion recovery program here. You can come and meet with our licensed counselors, who will help you along the journey toward forgiveness. It's never too late to find healing."

After thanking Liz for her kindness and willingness to hear her story, Jade leaned close and whispered, "Don't worry—I'm definitely not going to get an abortion. I'll stay in touch."

From that moment on, Jade was a regular at the pregnancy center. She began to recognize the unhealthy pressure her boyfriend placed on her and gained the strength to end their relationship. She found new housing, signed up for pregnancy and parenting classes, and began attending the center's after-abortion recovery program.

After the birth of her child, Jade plans to become a volunteer at the pregnancy center, where she hopes to be a courageous example to other women who find themselves navigating similar difficult decisions.

What Does It Mean to Be Pro-Life?

Being pro-life means being *for* life—for every life, including the lives of women, men, moms, dads, babies, toddlers, and teens. It's being *for* families and building a healthy, thriving culture. Approaching the issue of unplanned pregnancy with love and compassion opens doors and creates conversations in a way that judgment and shame never could. Offering resources, education, and support empowers women and men to make life-affirming decisions for themselves and their children.

As shown in the story of Jade's experience with Liz, being pro-life actually means being pro-woman in a holistic way: caring for a woman's physical and emotional state, her relationships, her livelihood, her future, and any needed healing from her past. Being pro-life can be expressed through simple yet powerful action.

> Approaching the issue of unplanned pregnancy with love and compassion opens doors and creates conversations in a way that judgment and shame never could.

In Jade's story, a short text—a reminder of someone willing to be present, to listen, to care—saved an unborn life and empowered Jade to overcome multiple obstacles to become a thriving, hopeful individual. Contrary to cultural assumptions, the pro-life view actually agrees with the pro-choice side in the belief that women's lives are valuable and worth supporting. We disagree, however, that a woman and the unplanned unborn cannot thrive simultaneously.

It's heartbreaking to know that a single abortion affects many lives in harmful, long-lasting, and often unacknowledged ways. We want to acknowledge the struggles, the pain, the fear, and the trauma as we firmly lean on the hope offered through pro-life ministries. As you will see throughout this book, there are countless creative ways that pro-life organizations and individuals help women and men by providing real choices that do not result in loss of life. Life and choice do not have to be in opposition to each other.

The Stories You'll Read

In the coming chapters, you'll read raw, honest stories of women who faced what felt like insurmountable adversity in their choices for life. These stories were collected from pregnancy resource centers across the nation and through personal interviews with the authors. The accounts reflect the experience many women have when facing an unplanned or unwanted pregnancy: An unexpected positive pregnancy test increases the complexity of a woman's life as she is confronted with making unplanned decisions. Her stress points often feel completely overwhelming, and the pressures she faces may increase fear and loneliness. These factors, along with the strong sway of culture, pull her down a convincing path toward the belief that abortion is *the* solution to a woman's life and success.

We divided the book into sections corresponding to the three major influences on a woman's decision—circumstantial difficulties (or economics), relational pressure, and holistic health. Each of the first three sections opens with a story to provide a visual that weaves together many hardships, stresses, or concerns that will be further explained in the chapters of that section. A woman's consideration of abortion is often complex and the pressures multifaceted. Through story, we want to help you understand how nuanced a woman's choice can be when she faces an unplanned pregnancy. The fourth and final section provides practical, compassionate action steps for you and your church.

After personalizing the concerns through dramatized accounts, we will present helpful information from at least one organization that addresses that particular pressure. Chapters include action steps and ideas about how you and your church can participate in pro-life work before ending with a devotional and an invitation for God to increase our compassion and broaden our ministry.

Equipping the Church

The book you're holding now was forged from the desire to help the church understand the struggles a woman faces, depoliticize the issue of life, and build empathy so local churches can better get involved and serve their communities. We will provide tangible next steps and ideas for you to act on and make a difference. You could be like Liz, who simply reached out to say, "I'm here for you." Being pro-life doesn't always require extravagant expression; her little text made all the difference for Jade. Even a simple action can create a chain reaction that transforms and saves a life. The faith community is uniquely gifted to offer real support, but most importantly, it offers the hope, healing, and wholeness found in Christ alone. As you read, be open to how God may invite you to speak out and take action in your specific sphere of influence.

Even a simple action can create a chain
reaction that transforms and saves a life.

We invite you to expand your heart to reflect the heavenly Father's compassion both for those who face unplanned pregnancies and for those who live with the regret of an abortion. This may even mean receiving forgiveness and unplanned grace for yourself, a friend, or a family member. Since no one is beyond the lavish love of God, we invite you into experiencing it and sharing it with others.

We hope the brave women's stories we've collected will show that while choosing life is not always easy—abundant, thriving life is possible through compassion and grace.

Shannon and Rachel's Story

"I just don't know," Shannon said to her friend Rachel.

"We've been over this so many times. I don't want to do it either, okay?" Rachel said.

Rachel was intent on her decision, and her level of agitation was building alongside Shannon's level of uncertainty. Shannon could sense the tension between her and Rachel reaching its breaking point. Out of fear of damaging their friendship, Shannon decided to keep her doubts to herself.

Shannon and Rachel had been best friends through college, and in the many ups and downs of post-college life, they grew to become more like sisters. They had vowed to support each other through thick and thin, and right now things were thin. Just a few months after graduation, they both found themselves working jobs that barely paid the rent. Neither woman had money to spare—and certainly not to support the babies they were carrying. How they both ended up pregnant at the same time, well, maybe that's something they could have laughed about in a different season, but neither of them found it amusing now.

Shannon had been dating her boyfriend, Owen, for a only few months when she discovered she was pregnant. He was out of the picture now. As for Rachel, her baby's father was never really in the picture at all. She hadn't told Shannon his full name because it was only a fling, something she just wanted to forget.

Rachel, always the practical one, believed that "facts don't care about your feelings." This philosophy drove her entire thought process. As she wrestled with her decision, she followed a very basic line of logic: A baby costs money, and there's no money. A baby needs a family, and there's no family.

"Plus," Rachel told Shannon, "we have our whole lives ahead of us."

Before she knew it, Shannon found herself in the clinic's waiting room, sitting next to Rachel.

The questions *How did I get here? What am I doing? Are there any other options?* reverberated in Shannon's mind.

Rachel sat still, but Shannon just couldn't. The stress of her doubt was taking a physical toll on her as she felt her chest tighten and her body grow shaky.

"None of this feels right," she finally said to Rachel.

"We've talked about this a hundred times," Rachel whispered with exasperation. "We can't afford kids. This is the logical decision. But we're in this together, so we'll get through it together."

This time, though, their back-and-forth was interrupted by someone. Shannon hadn't even noticed the security guard standing by the door, just a few feet away from where they sat.

"I hope you can excuse my overhearing, ladies, but if you're not sure about your decision, I just thought you should know that there are some people outside who might be able to help you if you want to talk to them," he said. "They've got a bus here that provides free pregnancy testing and ultrasounds."

As usual, Rachel was quick to answer. "No, I'm fine. I know what I'm doing," she said firmly, folding her arms and turning away from the man.

The security guard's eyes lingered on her for a moment, somewhat unconvinced. He then turned to Shannon. His gentle eyes struck a place deep inside her fears, somehow giving her courage.

"Outside?" she asked him.

"It's a brightly colored medical van. You can't miss it, but I can take you there myself if you'd like," he said to her.

All he offered was to walk beside her, but Shannon almost burst into tears as she stood up. He opened the door, and she turned back to look at Rachel, who remained defiantly stoic in her chair and wouldn't even look in her direction. Shannon thanked the security guard for offering his support.

Shannon tentatively approached the staff on the sidewalk near the bus. She was welcomed, given paperwork, and asked questions to assess her situation. Head down, eyes low, she told her story to the sonographer and social worker, who listened intently. Shannon's insecurity was obvious to the women on the bus, who looked for every opportunity to make her feel loved.

"You probably hear this sort of thing all the time," she said, feeling less than unique and bracing for them to brush past her story in the way people do when they're busy with something important.

But the social worker and nurse kept looking into her eyes and nodding, paying attention to her every word. Shannon began to feel more distinct, loved, and heard.

"Would you like to see your baby?" the nurse asked Shannon.

She nodded and lay down on the table for an ultrasound. Within moments, "it" became "he." He was a boy, already twenty-two weeks along. He had his whole life ahead of him. Suddenly Shannon's mind was singing with all the possibilities of what her life might be with him in it.

The social worker could see Shannon was caught in a pent-up flood of emotion. In that moment, she struggled to identify whether the tears running down Shannon's face were happy or sad.

"There are lots of people who want to help you, and I can connect you with them," the social worker assured her before listing off resources.

The grip of fear and helplessness that had held Shannon rigid and terrified for months slowly loosened. "I had no idea."

"That's why we're here," the social worker said.

Shannon stepped off the bus with new hope, ready to embrace her new life and excited to face the future knowing she was not alone.

She saw Rachel walk out of the clinic and ran to her, thinking it had only been about thirty minutes since she had left her. To her surprise, it had been two hours.

Shannon met Rachel in a sort of frantic joy, bursting with her new story, "The women over there helped me! I'm going to keep my baby!"

The words poured from her like a rapidly flowing river until she saw Rachel's swollen eyes. She knew her friend well enough to see her heart of sadness and regret. Her joy dwindled as the realization dawned on her. "You went through with it," Shannon said.

"We were in this together," Rachel cried in a mix of anger and sorrow. Shannon hugged her, unable to do anything else.

"I'm sorry. You were only doing what you thought was best. You didn't know." Everything Shannon could think to say sounded hollow in light of the contrast between what they were feeling. They stood in the parking lot, crying together yet now worlds apart.

Chapter 1

Pregnancy Resource Centers

The Forefront of Empowering Women to Choose Life

Pregnancy resource centers (PRCs) exist to provide options and aid to women facing unplanned pregnancies. Recall Shannon's story: she boarded the mobile medical unit thinking she had to do everything on her own. That's what most women think, and that weight is overwhelming.

My body, my choice, my responsibility.

PRCs help shift that narrative. The pro-life community wants women to know that while it is ultimately their choice to make and their lives to live, they don't have to bear all their burdens—whether financial or emotional—alone.

Shannon was able to choose life for her child after hearing about all the support available to her through her local pregnancy center. Perhaps the most striking element of her story, though, is the eventual contrast between the two women who walked into the abortion clinic together that day. The meeting place between such joy and such sorrow is extremely bittersweet. The PRC staff was not able to meet Rachel prior to her decision to terminate her pregnancy; however, the story does not end with her choice to abort. The pregnancy center offered care to her too.

The mission of every pregnancy center is to care not only for those *who choose life*; it is to care for women and men—period. God calls us to care, not based on the choices people make but based on the intrinsic value of their personhood.

Many pregnancy centers offer free after-abortion counseling services for individuals who, like Rachel, are walking through pain and need to heal. (We will tell you more about this unique ministry in chapter 10.)

Abortion advocates claim that abortion is a triumph of women's rights, freedom from the burden of motherhood. Perhaps this is true for some women; we respectfully leave room for the possibility that some feel unaffected by abortion. But the reality is that many women, like Rachel, are deeply broken by their choice to abort. And they deserve a voice as well.

> The mission of every pregnancy center is to care not only for those *who choose life*; it is to care for women and men—period.

As we learn about the essential role of pregnancy resource centers, why they're important, and how they help women navigate their real choices, we're going to look at some true stories. Real experience often reminds us of the humanity behind the hypothetical arguments.

Gabi described her unplanned pregnancy and interaction with her local PRC in an interview with the authors in 2019. Hers is just one example of many showing how centers help moms and save babies.[*]

---

[*]   Watch Gabi's story at UnplannedGraceBook.com.

Gabi's Story

Gabi was sitting on the bathroom floor of a friend's house when she confirmed she was pregnant. They'd just left a bar and, on a whim, stopped at a drugstore to pick up a pregnancy test.

"I had been feeling weird but didn't really think it could be true," she said.

She decided to check—just to be safe. As soon as the two lines appeared, she started sobbing. At the time, it felt like the worst news she could have ever received.

Gabi recalled, "I was in and out of bars, getting drunk. I wasn't ready to have a child. I was not even able to take care of myself, let alone another human being."

She put off deciding whether or not to continue her pregnancy for a few weeks. Then her friend told her about Matrix LifeCare Center, a pregnancy resource center in their town that provides free pregnancy tests and ultrasounds. Early one morning, she drove to Matrix.

Amy Hutchcraft is the client care director at Matrix. She said, "From the moment she walked in, I knew Gabi was upset. But I felt like we had a connection."

Because of this connection, Gabi confided in Amy, admitting she wasn't sure what she wanted to do with her pregnancy. Gabi wavered between abortion and parenting and was still unsure when she left the office that day.

But Amy didn't give up.

"She didn't have anyone to talk to. I wanted to be that person for Gabi, cheering her on," Amy said. "I wanted to make sure she knew that she was loved and that she had value and was courageous for sharing what she shared with me."

Amy invited Gabi to come back for an ultrasound. Gabi accepted and seemed excited. She asked Amy to come into the room as the registered nurse performed the ultrasound. Both women answered all of Gabi's questions, ensuring she understood everything she saw.

"[The ultrasound] was amazing. It's like a whole new light came into my life when I saw him for the first time. My heart got so warm in my chest, and I felt these tingles. I said out loud, 'Oh my God. There he is!' I just knew he was a boy," Gabi remembered.

During her pregnancy, Gabi received four ultrasounds at Matrix LifeCare Center and was able to take photos home to share with her family. Her final ultrasound before her due date was in their mobile medical unit (MMU).

"It was crazy!" she said. "The bus was out-of-this-world awesome. It's like nothing I've ever seen before. They had a TV and a bed—the whole setup. We got [my son] on the TV, and all of a sudden his hand went up and he waved at us. We all got so excited and screamed. It was so awesome. I'll never forget that day."

"Seeing my son completely turned my life around, like, a whole one-eighty," Gabi said with eyes full of hope and joy. "I started doing my prenatal care, I did the Baby and Me Tobacco-Free program and quit smoking, and I started my parenting classes."

"I was doing my parenting classes every week, and I couldn't wait to go," Gabi said. "Amy would sit with me, and we'd watch a video and do activities. I could ask her questions, and she always had the answer to every question. The classes were amazing, and every week I could pick out something new for the baby from the Nest [the center's baby clothing boutique]. The Nest is amazing, and they have everything: clothes, diapers, blankets, shoes. I even got supplies for my crib that I didn't know existed."

At eight months pregnant, Gabi decided to seek alternative housing. She didn't want to bring her son into a toxic and emotionally abusive home.

"Amy gave me a list of resources for housing. She helped me a lot through that."

Gabi found better housing just before her son's due date.

Before going to the hospital for the birth, Gabi recalled, "Amy made me a newborn checklist. She made me a hospital checklist and made sure I had everything. If I needed [a resource] that wasn't at Matrix, she got it for me. She was with me every step of the way. I wouldn't have made it through without her. I probably still couldn't, to this day, [make it] without her and Matrix," Gabi said.

In a gift basket for Gabi, Amy included a handwritten card stating, "We're here for you. We're a family." Those were not mere words; Amy's care reflected their sincere meaning.

Gabi gave birth to her son, Braxton, in October 2018.

"When I saw him, everything just stopped. I didn't hear or see anyone else. I kept my eyes right on him the whole time. Everything in the whole world shut down. I felt him and he clung on to me. It was the best feeling in the whole world," she said. "I fell in love for the first time in my whole life."

After the birth, Amy reminded Gabi that if she ever felt any postpartum depression and needed to talk, she was there for her.

"I was doing okay until the third week. Then it hit me like a brick," Gabi said, describing her depression. "I didn't want to be around anybody. I went to Amy, and she reassured me that it's okay to feel that way. It's normal, and we would get through it together. It was hard at first, but Amy really helped me get through that depression."

"Two years ago, I was spending all the money I made at the bar, getting drunk and doing stupid stuff. But now I'm a mom. I love being at home with [my son]. He is the best thing I could have in my life—hands down."

"Every time I go to [Matrix], it's very inviting and welcoming. Amy and every staff member know me by now. I've been going there for such a long time; they know who I am, and they're always so happy to see Braxton. I feel like I'm really part of their family now. I love them and they love me."

Tangible Support

Pregnancy resource centers assist individuals, like Gabi, in communities across the United States. A pregnancy resource center is a nonprofit organization that specializes in helping women and men facing an unplanned pregnancy understand all their options before making a life-altering decision. All PRCs are pro-life and do not refer for abortions. Formerly these centers were known as crisis pregnancy centers, but to remove the stigma of pregnancy as a crisis, the name was changed to more accurately reflect what these centers provide: pregnancy resources.

An analysis by the Charlotte Lozier Institute, the research arm of the Susan B. Anthony List (a network of pro-life individuals and organizations seeking to abolish abortion), found that in 2019:

- Pregnancy centers provided almost two million people with free services, with an estimated community cost savings of at least $270 million annually.
- Nearly three thousand centers nationwide provided vital services including medical services, parenting programs, and sexual risk avoidance education.
- More than ten thousand licensed medical workers provided care as staff and volunteers.
- More than 120 mobile medical units with ultrasound were on the road to take services to women in their communities.

- 79% of pregnancy centers offered free ultrasounds (up from 76% in 2017).
- 486,213 hours of free services were contributed by credentialed nurse sonographers and registered diagnostic medical sonographers.[1]

If a woman needs resources beyond what her PRC provides, the center will refer clients to various welfare programs for assistance. The United States currently has six major welfare programs: Temporary Assistance for Needy Families (TANF), Supplemental Nutrition Assistance Programs (SNAP), Supplemental Security Income, Earned Income Tax Credit, Housing Assistance, and Medicaid. Tamra Axworthy, the executive director of A Caring Pregnancy Center in Pueblo, Colorado, said her staff will often refer clients to TANF, Medicaid, and Women, Infants, and Children (WIC), which is a special supplemental nutrition program.

While pregnancy centers typically operate independently and are community and state-specific, most fall under the umbrella of a few national groups: Heartbeat International (www.heartbeatinternational .org), Care Net (www.care-net.org), and the National Institute of Family and Life Advocates (NIFLA, https://nifla.org). As of May 1, 2021, Heartbeat International estimates that 2,800 pregnancy center locations worldwide are affiliated with their organization alone.[2]

There are two categories of pregnancy resource centers based on the type of care they offer:

Nonmedical
     pregnancy tests
     options counseling
     parenting classes
     baby supplies
     sexual risk avoidance education

Medical (in addition to the above services):
> registered nurses and ultrasound technicians
> sexually transmitted infection (STI) testing and
> sometimes treatment

Nonmedical PRCs

Offering free pregnancy support to women, nonmedical centers provide self-administered pregnancy tests to their clients, who then each read the result with a staff member, known as a client advocate. The staff, or trained volunteers, provide options counseling as the women navigate their feelings and options based on their test results.

The client advocate will discuss with the client which of three options—parenting, adoption, or abortion—she is considering for her pregnancy. Depending on the client's response, the client advocate will ask her if she is open to more information about her options.

Through medically accurate brochures, videos, or other media, the client learns what she might experience when choosing any one of these three options. The client advocate provides an opportunity for the client to ask questions and offers her resources (brochures or online links, depending on her preference) related to the information they covered together. If the client is considering a particular option, her advocate can make arrangements for her to talk with someone, such as an adoption social worker. Since the conversation is heavy and urgent, the client advocate will often ask for permission to pray with the client. If the client is willing to receive prayer, staff will also approach the topic of faith and, if she's open, introduce the client to the gospel and connect her to a local church.

In addition to testing and counseling, PRCs provide parenting classes and other practical instruction to parents. Earn While You Learn is a popular curriculum that centers use to teach new and expectant moms and dads valuable parenting skills. These courses cover information from what to expect during pregnancy to fatherhood. They also offer practical education on topics such as budgeting or buying a home. As clients in the program complete the lessons or keep appointments with their client advocates, they earn "Mommy Money" or "Baby Bucks" to spend at the PRC's baby boutique. These stores are stocked with new donated items including baby clothes, maternity clothing, diapers, formula, car seats, strollers, cribs, and more.

Typically a client receives support and material resources from a pregnancy center for up to two years after her pregnancy. According to the Charlotte Lozier Institute, nearly three hundred thousand men and women attended parenting courses through PRCs across the nation in 2019.[3]

Many centers offer an online program called BrightCourse. Similar to Earn While You Learn, these classes can be tailored to the needs of each client, with information on pregnancy, infancy, toddlers, parenting, life skills, and more. New lessons are added each month and are accessible to PRCs.

Heidi Hill, the CEO of Birth Choice in San Marcos, California, uses BrightCourse to support her clients.

"The moms are able to schedule appointments when the baby is down for a nap or when dad is home. Travel expenses are reduced, and they are still able to accrue points for items in our boutique," she explained. "The moms and the client advocates have all benefited from using BrightCourse through a more effective use of everyone's time. We have had clients choose life without an ultrasound as a result of BrightCourse."

Another way PRCs engage their communities is by providing sexual risk avoidance education in local schools. Topics can range from healthy relationships, to respect, to family, to boundaries and communication. The classes inform students of the resources and additional support they can find at their local pregnancy center (more details in chapter 7).

Medical PRCs

In addition to everything a nonmedical pregnancy resource center provides, a medical PRC employs registered nurses or ultrasound technicians who are trained to perform sonograms under the guidance of a licensed medical director.

All medical PRCs rely on applicable national and state medical standards and licensing requirements. These PRCs operate under the oversight of a medically licensed physician who ensures standards of medical excellence are met. These centers can also be referred to as pregnancy resource *clinics* because they have licensed clinical staff including nurses and sonographers. The staff may also include licensed counselors and social workers with additional services to assist women in overcoming difficult life circumstances.

Using ultrasound technology to introduce an abortion-vulnerable woman to her child was pioneered by NIFLA in the mid-1990s.[4] This tool alone saves thousands of lives each year as the baby's life wins the heart of the mother and often changes her decision.[5] Early first-trimester ultrasounds use what is called "M-mode," which shows the wavelength of a fetal heartbeat and can be used to determine the gestational age of the baby. Ultrasounds in the second and third trimesters often utilize Doppler technology, which allows the mother to hear the rhythm of her child's heartbeat and watch the baby's movements.

Clinics offer a relatively large spectrum of services and care; however, each pregnancy center is unique in the services it offers. Some medical pregnancy clinics offer screening and treatment of STIs or have a full health clinic to offer prenatal care to clients. Everything offered at a PRC, both medical and nonmedical, is completely free to the client (with some exceptions for STI services, depending on the clinic). These services and supplies are subsidized by the generosity of individual donors and grants.

Pregnancy centers that wish to extend their services into their communities often do so through the use of mobile medical units. These buses are built either by Save the Storks or ICU Mobile. By going mobile, a pregnancy clinic can take the lifesaving resources of free ultrasound and pregnancy tests (and sometimes STI testing) to the places where abortion-vulnerable women are. The mobile medical units eliminate transportation inconvenience to women by parking near colleges, at shopping centers, in rural communities, or by abortion clinics. (All the stories in this book were acquired through pregnancy centers that met their clients on board mobile medical units built by Save the Storks.)

The heart of every staff member at a PRC is to help each woman thrive and make the best, most well-informed choice she can—to give her baby life and find a happier and healthier life for herself. The goal is to help clients break the cycle of unwed pregnancies, understand their value, and ultimately find healing and wholeness in Jesus Christ.

> We are blessed to provide love, support,
> and encouragement for all women, no
> matter their pregnancy decision.

Support for Individuals after Abortion

In addition to these programs, many PRCs offer after-abortion healing resources, classes, and counseling services. In 2017, pregnancy centers saw 24,100 clients for after-abortion support. Both men and women received support, counseling, and referrals to professional help when appropriate.[6]

Morgan came on board a mobile medical unit for her pregnancy test, then scheduled another appointment for her ultrasound. She brought her boyfriend to the second appointment, and the ultrasound determined she was six weeks along. They were truly conflicted about what to do and spent time talking about each option and what life would look like for them depending on which choice they made.

The couple made another appointment at the clinic and met with a licensed counselor who gave them the opportunity to share their honest feelings about their options.

When the clinic followed up with Morgan a few days later, she revealed that she had undergone an abortion. She admitted that the experience was more painful—physically and emotionally—than she had expected.

The pregnancy center invited Morgan to join them for after-abortion counseling. She agreed and has been encouraged by the freedom she feels to be honest about her pain and to find healing from her past.

The staff member who helped Morgan said:

> Society tends to portray abortion as an easy, quick fix with no regrets. Research shows us that is just not true. We are blessed to provide love, support, and encouragement for all women, no matter their pregnancy decision.
>
> When a pregnant woman enters our door, there are two lives that need tending. We mourn the loss of one life when a woman chooses abortion, but we are still committed to the care of the mother's life and pray the best for her as she travels the road to after-abortion recovery.

Both Gabi's and Morgan's stories display the heart of staff members in pregnancy resource centers across the nation. The staff and volunteers at these centers and clinics are ready and willing to walk alongside a woman no matter the outcome or her choice. They remind a woman that she is strong, capable, and empowered. To find the source of strength, staff will introduce their client to the truth of the gospel and show her how Jesus can bring her toward a successful, whole, healed, and empowered life.

As you read, you'll see again and again how vital pregnancy centers are. Staff members genuinely become family to women who once felt alone and afraid, certain they had no option other than abortion. But over and over you'll observe that when a woman is loved as an individual, she recognizes not only that her is life valuable but that her baby's life has value too.

Pregnancy resource centers seek to care for the Gabis, Shannons, Morgans, and Rachels of the world with love, compassion, and action. They provide care to women no matter the circumstances in order to help them.

Section 1

Circumstantial Difficulties

How Economic Difficulties Can
Impact a Woman's Choice

Rosliany's Story

In 2015, Rosliany arrived in Silver Spring, Maryland, from Venezuela. She was one of the millions of people who fled the country to escape severe food and medicine shortages, hyperinflation, and political unrest. She had studied to be a surgical nurse, but no one was hiring, so she left to find work and a better life in the United States.

"The idea of pursuing my objectives, my ideals, as a human being, as a woman, seemed so incredible in the beginning," she said.

She lived with an acquaintance as she established her life. After a while, she met a man whom she hoped to marry and decided to move in with him. A few months later, she discovered she was pregnant.

Rosliany immediately began searching online for the prices of abortions in her area. She found a clinic that charged $800. Unsure if she could afford the abortion, Rosliany kept scrolling through her options. "Free pregnancy test and ultrasound" caught her eye. It was an ad from the Centro Tepeyac Women's Center. She called the pregnancy center and made an appointment to meet the staff a few days later on a mobile medical unit near her house.

At her first appointment, she met Mariana, the executive director of the center at the time, and told her the situation she faced. In addition to her unexpected pregnancy, her boyfriend had just broken up with her and kicked her out of the house, and her visa had recently expired, so immigration officers had placed a tracking device on her ankle. She was essentially homeless and likely facing deportation.

"When I first met her, she voiced her concerns and how she was not ready to have the baby; she was not ready to be a mother. Her circumstances were some of the hardest I've seen," Mariana said.

Rosliany still decided to do an ultrasound that day. Right there in the middle of the screen, she saw her child for the first time and marveled at the life. She chuckled as the baby seemed to be performing calisthenics, as if on an aerobics video, and she could feel her own heart pounding as she watched the rhythm of the M-mode tracing the baby's heartbeat. But Rosliany found it hard to match the joy and excitement of the PRC staff surrounding her. The realities she faced were too overwhelming.

She left the mobile clinic, shoulders sagging with the concerns and fears weighing on her mind. Her deportation trial was scheduled for a month before her due date, and there was a very real chance she would be forced to return to a country where starvation was an actual possibility. It seemed cruel to bring a baby into such a world just to see it die from hunger. As a nurse herself, Rosliany wanted to ensure a good quality of life, especially for her own child.

Due to her immigration status, Rosliany couldn't work, and her resources were rapidly dwindling. Her Venezuelan family was in a far worse economic crisis, so she knew she couldn't ask them for help. She had an ever-present device on her ankle, reminding her that everything in her future was uncertain.

The PRC staff refused to give up on her challenging situation. They referred her to a local lawyer who resonated with Rosliany's situation. His own mother had moved to the United States when he was a child, and someone had helped them through the immigration process. He offered to take her case pro bono.

In addition to the attorney's support, a local church stepped in to help her with housing. Reflecting on that moment, Rosliany said, "I felt that God wasn't abandoning me. God was with me."

She moved in with a woman from the church named Maria, who provided a simple and comfortable room for her. Beyond that, Maria herself filled the whole house with a love Rosliany hadn't seen before. Staying in her home felt enchanting, honest, and restful.

For the first time, Rosliany felt like she had a moment to actually stop the dizzying speed of her troubling circumstances and think about her options.

If I choose this baby, we may be deported just a month after the delivery. If we're deported to Venezuela, we might both die of starvation. I can't watch my baby starve. That would be such a terrible death. Plus, I can't pay for medical bills. Her thoughts turned to her other option. *If I terminate this pregnancy, then I wouldn't have to watch him die if we're deported. And it would be one less thing I have to worry about as I face court. I don't have the money now, but I can try to save up enough to get that $800.*

At Rosliany's next appointment at the pregnancy center, she honestly expressed all the tormenting thoughts that had plagued her since her positive pregnancy test. After reviewing her options and addressing all her concerns, Mariana directed her to Catholic Charities and the Health Department, which offer assistance for those who cannot pay for critical health care.

With the added support systems found through the pregnancy center, church, and attorney, Rosliany committed to choosing life for her child. The future didn't exactly look bright, but a small twinkle of hope was starting to shine.

Her pregnancy continued without mishap until the thirty-first week. At her prenatal-care checkup, the doctor became extremely concerned.

"You have very high blood pressure," the doctor warned. "We need to monitor you closely to make sure your life and the life of your child stay safe."

Rosliany was admitted to the hospital. Her blood pressure medication wasn't working, and her life was in danger. The doctors and nurses quickly rolled her bed into the operating room to perform an emergency cesarean. The premature baby boy was born at thirty-two weeks and immediately taken to the NICU. Half-awake, Rosliany prayed, *God, help me be strong. Help my son stay strong.*

When her mind cleared from the anesthesia, she saw an extra medical band lying on the table. The ICU nurse explained, "That allows for one person to access your room and your son. Typically it goes to the father or another family member."

After thinking for a moment, Rosliany turned to the nurse and asked her to find the card with the PRC's number in her purse. She asked her to call Mariana. They'd become dear friends and basically family through the months leading up to her delivery.

Mariana's kind voice warmed Rosliany's heart as soon as she heard her speak. "Can you come to the hospital?" Rosliany asked her.

"Of course! I'll be there soon," Mariana said without hesitation.

Mariana entered the hospital room with a brilliant smile. Rosliany extended her hand, which held the medical wristband.

"I want you to have this."

Tears streamed down Mariana's face; she knew this meant Rosliany was claiming her as family—offering her the right to be the nearest person to this new mother and her son. Mariana sat by her side in intensive care and made sure that she had everything she needed during her recovery.

Early in her pregnancy, the major factor that kept pressuring Rosliany to choose an abortion was her economic situation. Although she didn't have $800 for an abortion, she knew she couldn't pay the hospital fees if she chose life. The emergency cesarean, eleven days of hospitalization, and three weeks in the NICU created a bill Rosliany could never pay, but thankfully, it never became an issue. With the guidance of the PRC, Rosliany had signed up for an emergency program for pregnant women through the Health Department.

With this assistance and support from Catholic Charities, church members, and the PRC, Rosliany's economic concerns were removed. "Everything was free. I didn't pay anything," she said.

She finally felt hope.

"I'm going to name him Emmanuel because, though this has not been an easy road, I know that God has been with me and He will be with Emmanuel throughout his life too," Rosliany said.

On March 27, 2018, Rosliany signed the birth certificate and asked the pregnancy center sonographer who provided her first ultrasound to become Emmanuel's godmother. Looking at her son, she whispered, "You are the son I always wanted. I will do anything to make your life better, stronger, safer, and more secure than mine. You can live every day knowing that God is with you."

During her pregnancy and in the years since, Rosliany's attorney helped her obtain a work permit through her political asylum. "I'm legal to work in the USA, and now I'm just waiting for what the judge is going to say about my case," she said. "I'm still praying, but I don't have any more fears."*

———————

Like many women facing an unplanned pregnancy, Rosliany's story is complex. The factors that initially convince a woman that abortion is her best option are often practical. The following chapters highlight the major role that economic stress—inadequate finances or material resources such as housing and insurance—plays in a woman's pregnancy decision. When economic stress is alleviated, a woman feels more freedom to consider all her options. Through the resources provided by pregnancy centers and other local organizations, she is empowered to choose life.

———————

* Watch Rosliany's story at UnplannedGraceBook.com.

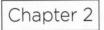

Chapter 2

Not Just Pro-Birth but Pro-Abundant Life

How Economic Resources Impact Women's Pregnancies

"No one wakes up thinking, I wish I could have an abortion today. They don't want that to be their only choice. We try to show them that it isn't their only choice, and if they want to parent, we will make sure that they have enough surrounding them to make it happen."

Sarah Jansen, social worker

Brienda was on her way to sign up for her sophomore classes at the local community college when she saw a mobile medical unit offering free pregnancy tests and ultrasounds. She was scared she might be pregnant but had been putting off a test for weeks, too afraid to know the truth. That day, though, she parked her car and walked toward the bus with her five-year-old daughter in tow. Within minutes, Brienda's fears were confirmed.

The world spun and tears blurred her eyes. She didn't want her daughter to know what was happening. How could she explain her reasons for abortion to her five-year-old? She didn't want to deal with the questions because, deep down, Brienda didn't think she could keep this baby. First, she needed to find a home away from her abusive boyfriend; then she had college to pay for and her daughter to think about.

The Issue Explained

Sarah Jansen, who serves as a social worker on the mobile medical clinic Brienda boarded, said, "Many women come to us wanting an abortion based out of fear. They feel they don't have enough money. They feel very alone."

In fact, the most common reason women choose abortion is financial. They don't think they have the resources or a support system to care for a child.

- The Guttmacher Institute, a pro-choice research group, found that 73% of women choose abortion because they feel they cannot afford a baby.[1]
- Guttmacher also found that about 75% of women seeking abortions in 2014 were poor or low income by federal standards.[2]

It's hard to argue with the financial reasoning that an abortion would be a lot less expensive than raising a child for eighteen or more years, especially when the one-time cost of an abortion is between $300 and $900 (depending on the trimester). The costs can be lower if the procedure is covered by insurance or inflated if the abortion takes place later in the pregnancy.

It's important to acknowledge the reality that living in poverty is incredibly difficult. If you are already barely making ends meet, the thought of providing for another person is beyond daunting. It feels impossible. In addition, the Urban Institute reported that living in poverty can cause extreme mental health issues:

> Poverty imposes a psychological burden so great that the poor are left with little mental "bandwidth" with which to perform everyday tasks.

> The constant anxiety and stress ... burn up
> cognitive capacity that could otherwise be used for
> productive activities.[3]

Living below the poverty line with unstable housing or work situations makes bringing a child into the world difficult. In fact, one of the biggest criticisms lodged by pro-choice advocates is that pro-lifers care about the baby only while it's in the womb but that they don't care about the circumstances it is born into or the financial situation of the mother. As James 2:15–16 says, "Suppose a brother or a sister is without clothes and daily food. If one of you says to them, 'Go in peace; keep warm and well fed,' but does nothing about their physical needs, what good is it?"

The accusation of not sticking around to help the mother provide for the child is simply false. Staff at PRCs are adept at networking and accessing local nonprofit resources—churches, food banks, clothing closets, the Salvation Army, the Gabriel Project, Catholic Charities, financial assistance programs, housing authorities, and others—to fully serve the needs of their clients. Each year, new programs are added to extensive networks to create even more robust support systems for individuals in need.

"We're not going to talk a woman into doing something really hard and then walk away," said Kelly Mapes, a sidewalk advocate for Alight Care Center in New York. "We're going to hook her up with resources and parenting classes and baby clothes. We're in her life as much as she wants."

Mapes's attitude reflects that of numerous pregnancy resource centers across the country that are connecting women to a wide variety of resources in their own communities. Through social workers, specialized care plans, parenting classes, and distribution of free material resources, it's safe to say that PRCs are working to help the entire family. Their efforts debunk the myth that pro-lifers care only about the baby.

> We're not going to talk a woman into doing something really hard and then walk away.

The Continuum of Care Advantage

One creative model of extensive support comes from Human Coalition's Continuum of Care (COC). Human Coalition is a network of pregnancy centers with a strategic plan to care for their clients. They don't just give their clients resources or referrals to outside programs and send them on their way—they walk with them every step of the journey.

Becky Craig, Human Coalition's national director of social services, was part of the team that developed the COC program. She realized that the clients who come to pregnancy centers are from so many different backgrounds and face so many distinct issues that the care each one needs has to be specialized.

When a woman is referred to the COC program, she first sits down with a social worker for an intake. Through this process, the coordinator can assess the unique challenges the woman is facing. Her needs can be anything from transportation, housing, a job, childcare, or pursuing her education. Together they develop a plan for the client to meet her goals, which may be related to health, career, education, finances, or relationships.

"Our ultimate hope is to help them get to a point where they feel comfortable choosing life," Craig said.

Once the client and social worker draft a plan, the COC coordinator accesses Human Coalition's electronic database of resources.

This is a network of organizations, mentors, government programs, and churches that have signed on to provide financial support, job training and placement, maternity housing, health care, and more.

"We vet all of our resources," Craig said. "In every area we have a clinic, we investigate all the places we refer to. We want to know what they provide and what the client needs to get the services."

Not only will coordinators give clients information on whom to call, they will also often accompany them to appointments and suggest the questions to ask. Additionally, they offer transportation, send them job leads, help craft résumés, or search for housing options.

"We do this because when you're already in a state of crisis, navigating these situations is even harder without someone to help you through it," Craig said.

Jas went to the Grapevine Women's Care Clinic—affiliated with Human Coalition—when she found out she was pregnant.

"They were so supportive," she said. "Even after I left, they sent messages asking how I was feeling and if I was okay. They helped remind me that I could do this. I didn't have to be scared. I knew I wasn't really alone. They understood that I was leaning toward abortion because I was scared, but they didn't judge me. They supported me the whole way through."

The clinic didn't just help Jas choose life, then send her away; they continued to walk with her through the COC model.

Jas continued: "They helped me find doctors and helped me know what I needed to do each month. They made sure I had my prenatal care. Every few weeks I came back for ultrasounds and they'd answer any questions I had. They basically held my hand through the whole process. I was pretty shocked, honestly, because I know they have other clients they work with, but they were always there to answer my texts and help me. They were like my personalized nurses."

The clinic also knew that Jas needed supplies, so they partnered with a local church to throw a baby shower, lavishing her with more love and support.

"They've been a helping hand the whole way through," Jas said. "My Continuum of Care coordinator is awesome. I've asked her to help me with schools, finding financial resources while I couldn't work, finding a better job, and just everything. She always responds quickly with 'No problem—I can do it' or 'Let me look that up for you real quick,' and she never says, 'No, I can't help.' I can ask one question, and she comes back with about fifteen options for a solution. Like when I said I wanted to go back to school to study nursing, she came back with multiple schools and the financial aid available for each one."

As Jas's story illustrates, even after a woman meets her goals through the Continuum of Care, the assistance continues.

"My [COC coordinator] still checks on me and my son. I send her pictures. She's part of my family, basically," Jas said. "The whole staff is so welcoming—they're all great. You can't have a bad day around them. They're just all amazing."

Human Coalition also has a mentorship program that pairs women with members from a local church to help them as they continue their journey in parenting and beyond.

"Understanding the emotional needs that a mom has is extremely powerful," said Kristin Holubk, a Continuum of Care coordinator at the Grapevine clinic. "We believe that's how you see chains broken—chains of poverty and abuse. It happens when people feel loved and cared for and known."

Craig echoed this by explaining Human Coalition's mission: "Reach, rescue, and restore. We want to reach expecting moms, rescue their babies, and restore their families."

Sarah Jansen, who was part of the team that helped Brienda at the beginning of the chapter, shares the same attitude at her pregnancy center in Iowa: "When you help women realize they are not alone and show them that the community has resources to help them, suddenly the reasons for an abortion don't seem like such a big hurdle."

PRCs are making an impact on moms and babies by connecting them to communities of people who step in to fill the gaps in their lives. They provide a more holistic example of what it means to be pro-life.

Eliminating Abortion and Poverty, One Life at a Time

Let Them Live (LTL) is another innovative organization seeking to help alleviate the temporary economic struggles of abortion-vulnerable women. When LTL founder, Emily Berning, recognized that most abortions happen because the mother is facing economic hardship, she decided to do something about it.

"Seventy-three percent of women choose abortion due to financial burden, and we exist to offer financial assistance so they can choose life instead," she explained.

LTL partners with Sidewalk Advocates for Life, whose staff talk with women on the sidewalks near abortion clinics. They also partner with pregnancy resource centers and Heartbeat International to reach pregnant women in economic crisis. Social media is an invaluable tool to inform struggling women about the resources at LTL as well.

When a woman seeks assistance with LTL, she is contemplating abortion because of financial stress. She cannot afford her child for at least one of a variety of reasons: she just lost her job, she's already struggling to pay rent, or the father of the child is pressuring her to abort and she relies on him for financial support.

"First we connect the woman to a PRC where she can get an ultrasound. We require the ultrasound as proof that she is pregnant. After meeting our criteria, we will help her financially for typically two to four months. We pay bills directly to the companies so there is no misuse or questions about the funds," Berning explained.

> When you help women realize they are not alone and show them that the community has resources to help them, suddenly the reasons for an abortion don't seem like such a big hurdle.

"We also have counselors who help each mom develop a budget and figure out a plan to get on her feet so she can wean herself off our full support," Berning continued. "At first, we pay 100 percent of her bills, but after a month or two, we will drop it to 75 percent and continue to drop it until the mom is comfortable and capable of paying her bills all on her own."

The intention is to help her become fully financially sufficient.

"Our goal in the end is not for them to be dependent on us for a long time. Often their obstacles are temporary, but in a financial crisis they think abortion is their only solution. We help them through the crisis and ensure they feel they're in control again."

One story Berning shared was of a homeless woman in California who found LTL online. Aporia lived in her car and was two days away from her abortion appointment. She reached out to LTL and told them that after her abortion she was going to commit suicide.

"I know I won't be able to live with myself," Aporia told them.

Although LTL is based in the Midwest, Berning and her husband immediately flew to California to offer personal support, which is something they're willing to do for any mom in a crisis situation.

"We just wanted to help her and make her feel like she's not alone. In-person support is so important," Berning explained.

Aporia decided to choose life with the knowledge that she could change her circumstances and that LTL was committed to helping her. They shared Aporia's immediate needs on their website, and many across the country—churches and both pro-life and pro-choice individuals—stepped up to assist. With their support, she found housing and developed a plan to provide for herself and her child in the future.

A few months went by, and the Bernings found themselves flying to California again, this time to be at Aporia's delivery. To their surprise, all the family members who had once pressured Aporia to abort now surrounded her in the hospital.

Aporia's dad offered Emily Berning a heartfelt "Thank you." Giving her a huge hug, he said, "You're now part of our family."

"There are real people who need our help, and we have a duty to help them," Berning said. "Our unspoken motto is from the movie *Schindler's List*," she continued.

Oskar Schindler was a German businessman during World War II who saved more than a thousand Jews by employing them at his factory as essential workers. In the closing scene, the Jews who worked for Schindler gave him a gold ring with these words inscribed in it: "Whoever saves one life saves the world entire."[4]

Berning concluded, "If we can save just one life from abortion, we can change the world—and that's what PRCs do every day."

Brienda's Story: Coming Full Circle

When Brienda boarded the mobile medical unit, she was scared, confused, and unsure whether she could take care of another child. Her living situation was unstable; she was totally isolated from family and financially insecure. With increasing feelings of loneliness and helplessness, Brienda was certain she had no other choice but abortion.

To her surprise, the pregnancy center offered support similar to the Continuum of Care program by connecting her with several community resources including educational scholarships, affordable housing grants, and food stipends to get her on her feet financially. With the security provided by their love and support, Brienda chose life.

Reflecting on the role of her PRC, Brienda said, "They were an ear if I ever wanted to talk. I felt like abortion was my only option … until I went to the pregnancy center. I felt alone and defeated at the time, but [the staff] gave me hope, encouragement, and support. They threw a baby shower for me and gave me diapers, wipes, and other necessary supplies."

Her choice to keep her baby gave Brienda an entirely new perspective on her own life.

"My son gave me the kick I needed," she said. "Having my son changed my life completely. He gave me the motivation and encouragement I needed to grow up. I stopped feeling sorry for myself and got up and started doing what I needed to as a mother. I chose not just life but a better life. To give my kids a better life, I had to give myself a better life too."*

When PRCs, churches, and communities work together, women's decisions for life are fully supported and their lives are eternally changed.

Wondering Where to Start?

Connect with your local PRC to determine how you and your church could support the clients they serve. Perhaps you or someone in your congregation could offer aid in the following ways:

---

*   Watch Brienda's story at UnplannedGraceBook.com.

- Host a baby shower and provide gifts to an expecting mom.
- Check out Let Them Live (www.letthemlive.org) to donate directly to a mom who needs temporary financial support.
- Offer mechanic or handyman services to fix vehicles or provide home repairs for those under financial stress.
- Provide interior decorating services to furnish a new apartment or nursery for a mom with housing needs.

Reflecting the Father's Heart

> The righteous will answer him, "Lord, when did we see you hungry and feed you, or thirsty and give you something to drink? When did we see you a stranger and invite you in, or needing clothes and clothe you? When did we see you sick or in prison and go to visit you?"
>
> The King will reply, "Truly I tell you, whatever you did for one of the least of these brothers and sisters of mine, you did for me." (Matt. 25:37–40)

Serving Jesus is not always glamorous. Helping people is messy and hard because we're all broken. Still, caring for others is how we express our love for our Creator.

As the last song in the musical *Les Misérables* states, "To love another person is to see the face of God."[5]

How can you express your love for God more fully to those in your community who feel far from the Lord?

Prayer

Father, broaden my capacity to love and serve You. Deepen my understanding of Your heart not only for me but also for those who are vulnerable and hurting near me. I acknowledge that everything I have comes from You, and I offer what I have to be used by You to help others. Ignite my passion to serve those who need healing, and draw those financially struggling to me and my church so we can share Your love with them in tangible ways. Thank You for being a good, generous Father. Help me reflect Your generosity to those who need it most. In Jesus' name, amen.

Chapter 3

The Importance of Housing

Maternity Homes, Short-Term Housing, and Equipping the Church to Open Its Doors to Those without a Safe Place

"The greatest love is the love of our neighbors. We have to start loving the people we're in community with."

Ken Norwood, COO of Safe Families for Children

"I have cash," Kendra said. "I can't have this baby, and I need to do this fast."

Without a second thought, the receptionist at an abortion clinic in Schenectady, New York, scheduled Kendra's abortion for the next day.

Kendra was new to the area. In fact, she had arrived on a bus just two weeks earlier, seeking safety from her partner who had recently become physically abusive. Her instinct to protect her daughters kicked in after her boyfriend hit her in a heated argument. With urgency, she told her five girls, "If it can't fit into your backpack, we can't take it."

Leaving her oldest daughter with her own mother to finish school, Kendra took her four younger girls on the long journey toward a better life.

But life wasn't necessarily easier here. Kendra and her daughters all slept on the same bed in a friend's spare room. With the clothes they had stuffed in their backpacks and little else, Kendra felt the pressure of providing for her family but didn't know where to begin. Before she could develop a new normal, Kendra started to feel ill. As she checked out of the local dollar store, something told her to buy a pregnancy test.

When she took it, to her shock and horror, two lines instantly appeared. Her heart raced as she searched online for "abortion clinics near me." Kendra wanted no additional reminders of her past, and her present situation didn't have room for another person. She was unemployed and practically homeless. Trying to find food for her four growing girls was burden enough.

Homeless and Pregnant

Kendra's story highlights a crucial need for women fleeing abusive relationships: safe housing. Many women feel pressure to remain in abusive relationships because they don't have access to housing or income aside from their partners. Because of fear of further abuse, abortion becomes the easiest choice because dealing with both abuse and a pregnancy is far too overwhelming. Knowing that stable and affordable housing is available can make all the difference in taking the step to leave a toxic relationship and make a choice for life.

In addition to abuse and an unstable home life, some women actually become homeless *because* of pregnancy. Their partners or parents may kick them out when they learn of the pregnancy.

Homeless women have higher rates of unplanned pregnancy than those who are housed. The reasons are rooted in a variety of issues ranging from mental health, rape, human trafficking, and limited resources to contraception, just to name a few. Because of the transient nature of homeless populations, accurate statistics can be difficult to track, but the US Department of Health and Human Services estimates that 6 to 22 percent of young homeless women may be pregnant.[1]

Covenant House, a nonprofit that serves homeless youth, reports an even higher number in a related statistic: "About 44 percent of young women and 18 percent of young men, ages 18 to 25, who face homelessness report being a parent or pregnant. Each year, hundreds of thousands of children—up to 1.1 million in the U.S. in 2017—live with a young mom or, less frequently, a young dad who is homeless."[2]

Access to Care

Pregnant women who are homeless have limited access to medical and prenatal care. Many face a series of mental health issues like depression and PTSD with no means of obtaining treatment. In a study published by the *American Journal of Orthopsychiatry*, one-third of young homeless women who had children in their care met the criteria for lifetime major depressive episode (MDE) and posttraumatic stress disorder (PTSD).[3]

These statistics are troubling and highlight the extreme vulnerability of pregnant or parenting moms who are homeless. Housing might be the most pressing thing a homeless woman needs, but it usually doesn't end there. Most also benefit from access to trauma therapy, drug and alcohol recovery, financial help, educational opportunities, and much more.

Maternity Homes

When a woman decides to carry her child, there is often a gap in supporting infrastructure to back her. Maternity homes provide a concrete response to the ongoing physical needs of pregnant women, beginning with a safe place to rest.

The concept of maternity homes has been around for generations, but their reputation is much improved from those of your grandmother's generation. In the past, parents would send their unwed pregnant daughter away to a maternity home to quietly have her baby and then place the child for adoption, sometimes against her will. The whole experience was shaming and secretive.

> # We know healing happens in the context of relationships and in community.

The purpose and experience of today's homes has broadened to empower moms in need of assistance during a difficult season. While they may range in size and level of support, maternity homes exist to provide housing and other needs for pregnant or parenting moms. These temporary shelters work to help women meet goals in areas such as education, employment, and financial stability. Rather than serving only as a place to host pregnant women until they can return to their normal lives, most maternity homes provide prenatal care, parenting classes, education support, and help with the adoption process.

Currently there are more than 450 maternity homes in the United States.[4] About a quarter of these homes are affiliated with Heartbeat International's National Maternity Housing Coalition (NMHC).[5] The NMHC group of maternity homes promotes life-affirming efforts and housing practices across the United States. They share best practices and efforts with one another and gain training and help to fulfill their individual missions.

Heartbeat International's NMHC housing specialist, Mary Peterson, explained that modern maternity homes have expanded their scope and services.

"The heart of it is working with pregnant women facing various circumstances," she said. "Maternity homes are a concrete response to the ongoing needs of pregnant women. Most women have made the decision to carry their child; they now need supporting infra-structure to back it up. Maternity home staff are thinking about her employment, education, long-term healing, and practical skills. It is a long-term response in the life movement."

Though all maternity homes typically provide some level of coun-seling services, life-skills training, and job or educational support, not all maternity housing looks the same. Here are four main models that exist today:

> **Live-in houseparents:** These homes house pregnant or parenting moms with "houseparents," or married couples who live in the home with the moms to provide daily help in the context of their family life.

> **Live-in staff:** Various staff members live with the moms on-site to develop relationships and establish a stable setting.

> **Shift staff:** Specially trained staff work in shifts and are hired for their specialized services (e.g., case management) to meet the needs of the women living at the home.

> **Host homes:** Organizations that screen host families and connect them to pregnant moms who need a place to live. These organizations also provide training and referrals throughout the expectant moms' stays.

Mary Peterson noted that many of the women living in maternity homes have faced tough home lives and even trauma.

"We're going to walk with someone for months or years even," she said. "We know healing happens in the context of relationships and in community—a home life where people are engaged and watching out for each other. That's where real healing work happens. Maternity homes show we care about the mom and the baby."

Healing through Housing

Originally Kendra was crashing at a friend's place, struggling to make ends meet for herself and her daughters. Her story could have ended very differently if her practical need for safe housing had not been met.

After she left the abortion clinic, with her appointment set for the following day, Kendra saw the Alight Care Center's mobile medical unit parked at the curb. Kelly, a volunteer with Alight, approached her with a warm smile and invited her to come on the bus for a free ultrasound.

Kendra was hesitant at first, but something about Kelly won her over. Plus, Kendra would need to know how far along she was for the abortion procedure the next day. The two women boarded the bus, and Ellen, the center's board-certified family nurse practitioner, gave her an ultrasound. As soon as the screen lit with the wavelength of her baby's heartbeat, Kendra burst into tears.

In that moment, Kelly looked at Kendra and reassured her: "You're not going to go through this alone."

The two women left the bus and went to a nearby coffee shop, where Kendra shared her full, heart-wrenching story with Kelly. Throughout their conversation, Kelly spoke words of encouragement. It began to sink in for Kendra that maybe she wasn't alone and maybe abortion wasn't her only option. From that moment on, Kelly was with Kendra every step of the way.

When Kelly heard about Kendra's living situation, she thought of a plan. It just so happened that she owned a real estate business and knew of an ideal house for Kendra's family. Understanding Kendra's financial stress, Kelly paid for the first few months of rent and ensured the house was furnished and filled with food, clothing, and other necessities for Kendra and her girls. The pregnancy center and a local church showered Kendra with baby supplies and became a second family in many ways.

Kelly's love, support, provision, and consistent kindness helped reignite the strength within Kendra. She rose to the occasion and determined to provide a thriving home for all her children.

By first meeting Kendra's practical needs of housing and financial aid, the church and pregnancy center helped inspire a hero. Kendra saved the life of her sixth daughter because she found a home away from home, a new family, and a hopeful outlook on life.[*]

Safe Families

Access to housing made all the difference in Kendra's story. Safe housing is vital to women facing an unplanned pregnancy, as well as to women needing an escape from an abusive relationship—something we will look at in the next section. The church is one of the best equipped, though often untapped, resources to tackle this problem. But many churches aren't sure where or how to start.

> When God's people care for others in the way He desires, the results transform culture and are a brilliant reflection of the Father's heart.

"The church naturally has people who are a little overwhelmed by how to make a difference, and they really want direction on how to make a lasting life-transformational impact," said Ken Norwood, the chief operating officer of the national nonprofit Safe Families for Children.

---

[*]   Watch Kendra's story at UnplannedGraceBook.com.

The organization involves churches in tangible ways to make a transformational impact on struggling moms and families. Churches can be particularly helpful for moms facing an unplanned pregnancy, similar to Kendra, who want to get on their feet but struggle since they already have kids to take care of.

As an alternative to the traditional foster care system, Safe Families provides temporary housing for children while their mothers seek help and stability. The organization helps a woman in an unplanned pregnancy by connecting her and her family to a community of people who first assist with her practical needs but also provide temporary care for her children. Best of all, Safe Families equips the church to be part of the process.

"The church is the root of everything for us," Norwood explained. "All training and recruitment happen through a local church. We believe the greatest mission field is literally across the street from the church—women struggling and those hurting in our community who need a helping hand. Biblical hospitality is our heartbeat."

Making the Connections

Pregnancy resource centers can refer a mom in need to Safe Families. For six weeks, her children will live in the home of a Safe Families host family while she regains stability. Before a child is placed in a host home, Safe Families assesses the host family to make sure it's a safe environment. All host families go through an application process, background check, and home study and provide references before they are cleared to take in children.

Once a child is placed, the host family will be surrounded with what they call "a circle of support." This provides them with access to a family coach and other staff from Safe Families.

Meanwhile, a team from Safe Families will surround the mom with her own circle of support, helping with whatever need she has. This could range from assisting with a job search or finding stable housing to looking for reliable transportation or connecting her to counseling.

The family coach supervisor will check in with both parties often. The mom facing difficulties will also be surrounded by a social worker and coach to help her stabilize while her child is being cared for.

"Parents will never lose custody in our program," Norwood continued. "The playing field is leveled in this model. Neighbors are helping neighbors. Our staff will help her job search, or if she needs a new car, they will help her find one. The goal is to love on the mom."

When children go into the foster care system, they spend an average of two years there. With Safe Families, a typical home stay is about six weeks. Additionally, 93 percent of children are reunited with their families, as opposed to just 50 percent in foster care.[6]

The Impact of the Church

In their seventeen-year existence, Safe Families has worked with more than 4,500 churches across the United States.

Knowing she has housing solutions opens up more options for a mother facing an unplanned pregnancy. These are the kinds of resources that can truly move a woman past the decision of abortion and into a place where raising a baby is possible.

"This is where the church needs to step up," Norwood said. "To be that holistic bridge in the pro-life space. It's not enough to just say, 'Life is worth it.' We have to say, 'We're going to help you. Yes, this is hard, but it shouldn't be scary.'"

Wondering Where to Start?
Maternity Homes

Heartbeat International has a directory of more than 450 maternity homes in the United States and beyond.

Search Heartbeat's worldwide directory (www.heartbeatservices.org/worldwide-directory) to find the nearest maternity home in your community and learn about the programs they offer. Figure out where you and your church can get involved, whether it's volunteering your time or donating money or other resources.

Become a Safe Families Church

Visit Safe Families for Children (www.safe-families.org) to see whether there is a local Safe Families chapter in your community. Or learn more about starting a chapter at your church. You can determine which of the three levels of involvement you want your church to take part in.

Reflecting the Father's Heart

Hospitality and caring for those who are most vulnerable in society are integral to the gospel and very near the heart of God.

When Israel found itself in Babylonian captivity, God spoke through the prophet Isaiah, calling His people to reengage with true religion.

> Is not this the kind of fasting I have chosen:
> to loose the chains of injustice
>   and untie the cords of the yoke,
> to set the oppressed free
>   and break every yoke?
> Is it not to share your food with the hungry
>   and to provide the poor wanderer with shelter—

> when you see the naked, to clothe them,
>> and not to turn away from your own flesh and
>>> blood? (Isa. 58:6–7)

God reminded Israel that He cares about the very practical, tangible expressions of obedience. When God's people care for others in the way He desires, the results transform culture and are a brilliant reflection of the Father's heart.

> Then your light will break forth like the dawn,
>> and your healing will quickly appear;
> then your righteousness will go before you,
>> and the glory of the LORD will be your rear
>>> guard. (v. 8)

As you consider the Father's heart for women who experience homelessness or the stress of unstable housing, ask the Lord to inspire you to know how you can make a difference.

Prayer

Father, thank You for welcoming me and preparing a place for me to be with You forever. Open my heart to help those who are without home or family as they face a pregnancy. Give me wisdom, guidance, and boldness to help in whatever way You call me to serve. I pray for those who do not have a home right now, that You would use me and use Your church across our nation and the world to provide for those in need. I ask that the beauty of Your hospitality would shine through the church and draw all people to Yourself. Help us, as the church, to be faithful to all You've called us to be. Amen.

Section 2

Relational Pressure

How Others Affect a Woman's Choice

Keilah's Story

"Oh my goodness, look at you!" Keilah's mother tried to hold back proud tears as she doted on her not-so-little girl. For the first time in a while, Keilah's mom was excited for her and delighted with her choices.

A few months earlier, Keilah's parents had been heartbroken when she broke up with her boyfriend, Brian, but this night felt like it might lead to a new beginning. No one in the family kept his or her feelings secret. Keilah's dad was the wrestling coach at school, and Brian had been one of his favorite students. Her mother treated him like a son, charmed by his fun personality. They all hoped that Keilah's acceptance of Brian's prom invitation would rekindle their relationship. None of them had any clue about the real test she had been facing. She couldn't bring herself to tell them the true reason she had broken up with Brian.

While they had been dating, Brian had constantly pressured Keilah to have sex with him. She was tired of refusing him and then dealing with his cold shoulder and pouting. She wanted a man who was committed to her for who she was, not for what she was willing to give sexually. After all, she was only seventeen. As unpopular as Keilah's stance was with her friends, she wanted to save sex for marriage. After their breakup, Brian became relentless about something else he wanted. He wanted Keilah to be his date for prom. She grew tired of putting up a wall. *What's one night?* she thought. She finally said yes.

Keilah never really felt like she had much say in her life. Her experiences reinforced the lies that she was worthless and, like Cinderella, should just serve others and keep out of the way. Her home was filled with violence. Any hint of disobedience was met with brutal beatings from her parents, which were fueled by the frustration they felt at their disintegrating marriage.

Prom night felt like an escape from her complicated life at home. Everyone was dressed up, dancing, and laughing together. Again, like Cinderella, it felt magical. For the first time in as long as she could remember, Keilah felt like she could let her guard down a little with Brian and have some fun, as friends.

Brian told Keilah he had something special planned for the after-party, so they cut out early from the school dance. Brian drove her out toward the beach and onto a secluded drive. They pulled up to a house that Keilah had never seen before.

"Where are we?" she asked.

"Don't ask so many questions!" Brian said with a playful laugh as he grabbed her hand and pulled her up the sidewalk toward the house.

When they went inside, Keilah expected to find a house full of friends, but she quickly realized she was alone with Brian—no lights, no music, no more magic—just his body pressed against her in the dark.

"I don't want to do this," she said, but Brian ignored her, knowing that her four-foot, eleven-inch frame was no match for his strength as a wrestler. Keilah didn't feel like a princess anymore. Her cries fell on deaf ears as her worst fear became reality. Brian wanted one thing, and he was going to take it, regardless of her wishes. The magic of prom night was over. Keilah became a victim of rape.

The next day, Keilah woke up in her bedroom at home, sickened by flashbacks and memories she wished she could erase. She felt stripped of her voice, unable to find the courage to tell her parents—or anyone else for that matter. Everyone loved Brian. Would they even believe her? And if they did, it would ruin so much for so many people. She wasn't ready for the fight or to face the pain that telling could bring on her.

To make things worse, her parents kept inviting Brian to the house and encouraging Keilah to spend time with him. She was reliving the trauma over and over in her own home, a place where she should feel safe. Where could she turn? She tried to talk with a friend, but she told her she would be "fine." As time went on, her shame and unresolved pain pushed her into emotional isolation. Her heart felt torn in too many directions to count.

Graduation came and went like a blur. It was meant to be a time of celebration, but instead, Keilah slipped into a deep depression. She tried to ignore what had happened to her and just continue on with her normal life, but she knew that something felt different, and it was more than just the trauma. She started waking up every morning feeling nauseated. Her friend who knew what had happened with Brian started joking with her, saying things like "Maybe you're pregnant! Wouldn't that be funny?"

Not revealing the fear she felt or the dread that seemed to fill her stomach, Keilah laughed along as her friend took her to buy a pregnancy test.

She didn't think her heart could sink any lower or that her fear could become greater until she saw two lines appear on her pregnancy test. Keilah's heart was in her throat. Question after question crashed like stormy waves in her mind, as the ocean had crashed against the shore at the beach house that night.

What am I going to do?

How should I tell my parents?

What if they kick me out?

How could I ever support this life when I haven't figured out how to support my own?

Brian had brought this storm into her life.

Keilah mustered the courage to tell Brian about her pregnancy. He said he would support her, but it soon became obvious that he would never actually be a father to their child—let alone support Keilah as a mother or a person. He was pursuing his own dreams of college and ignored the promises he'd made to Keilah.

Loneliness gripped Keilah to the core. She needed support, and though she was scared, she knew it was time to turn to her parents. The first thing out of her father's mouth was a series of harsh accusations.

"What did you do?" he asked, making it seem as if the rape had been her fault. It was three days before her mom spoke to her again, and when she did, her words were barbed with judgment.

After a week that felt like months, Keilah's father sat her down and finally spoke some calming words. "It's your body, Keilah. Do what you think is right."

Abortion was out of the question for Keilah. What Brian had done was wrong, but why should her child pay for it? "Maybe I should place the child for adoption," she reasoned. "I can't give her the life she deserves. I mean, what could I give her? I have nothing."

Her father's demeanor had been cold and stern, but Keilah saw his heart melting before her eyes. In a moment of tenderness, he looked his daughter in the eye and said, "Keilah, your love will be more than enough."

Uncertainty had been holding Keilah's heart hostage, but her father's words set her free and gave her the confidence she needed.

"Dad, I'm going to keep this baby. I'm going to take responsibility for her life. She deserves a chance to become someone."

Keilah found the courage to make her decision, but that didn't mean her pregnancy was easy. Judgment and shame were piled on her. Her parents told her not to speak about her pregnancy with her siblings and made her wear baggy shirts to hide her belly as it grew. The stress was taking a toll on her parents' already-rocky relationship as well. At night Keilah would lie awake in bed with her eyes closed, pretending to be asleep as her parents' raging voices echoed through the house. These episodes of arguing and violence between Keilah's mom and dad often stimulated contractions.

As the stress in their home mounted, Keilah also began to have nightmares. Her dreams were threaded with traumatic memories as she relived scenes from the beach house over and over in her sleep. Keilah's night terrors jarred her awake, sweating and with knife-like pain in her stomach. It was as if something were trying to destroy her from within. More and more often she found herself crouched alone on the bathroom floor, vomiting into the toilet—with no one to hold her hair back and tell her she would be okay. She was far from okay.

Finally, one month from her due date, the unexpected news of her grandmother's death pulled Keilah from the spell of her situation at home. It was only days before Christmas, when they would have spent quality time together again. Her grandmother was the one woman who made her feel unconditionally loved and safe. The shock of her death brought on contractions that grew more frequent and severe, until Keilah knew without a doubt that she was in labor.

The doctor looked concerned as he informed Keilah, "The placenta is broken, and your baby's heart rate is dropping quickly. We have to perform an emergency cesarean immediately, but there is a real possibility that you or the baby could die."

Lying on the operating table, in her last moments of consciousness, Keilah prayed, *God, we haven't been too close, but if You're going to take a life today, take mine. Make sure my daughter's life is protected.* Keilah drifted off with her prayer.

The distant sound of voices and the beeping of monitors slowly brought Keilah out of her sleep. She woke up in a room to other moms celebrating the arrival of their bundles of joy. Their beds were surrounded with balloons and flowers. Everyone else had visitors sharing in the excitement of new life. Keilah's story was different with no family to support her. But she sensed that God was there, and He made her strong.

With that strength, she looked into her daughter's face and quietly sang, "We're gonna be all right." There were no balloons, no celebrations—just a baby wrapped safely in her mother's arms. But somehow, in that moment, the world felt exactly as it should be.

She rested at the hospital as long as she could—until the nurse said it was time to gather her things and head home. She wished she had better insurance so she could've stayed another night and had one more peaceful night of rest.

Keilah held her daughter tightly as she entered her home for the first time as a mother. She wanted to protect her own child from the trauma she had experienced at far too young an age. Although they were initially greeted with excitement, it wasn't long before it wore off and things became just as Keilah had feared.

The physical abuse between her parents escalated and spilled over to her and her siblings. Keilah's mother was the one who instigated most of the violence at home. Ironically, the chaos caused by her mother drove her mother to walk out the door and never come back. Keilah felt relieved that her daughter would be safe from the violent outbursts.

After her mother left, though, their home continued to fall apart. Even though she had caused most of the trouble, Keilah's mom had held a lot of things together, especially the family business. It began to fail, and when it did, the family lost their home. Keilah found herself homeless, out on the streets.

Keilah's difficulties seemed to never end, but she was determined to fight on for her little girl. She located housing for herself and her daughter in the low-income area of town, where few positive stories ever emerged. She soon learned that seeking survival as a petite, interracial single mom came with many challenges, but Keilah had dreams to pursue. She'd always wanted to be a singer and often did gigs at local coffee shops and bars. It wasn't much, but she loved singing. Even if it didn't pay much, she had what she needed—her little girl and some big dreams.

Today her dreams are still a work in progress. Life is the good, the bad, the ugly, and the beautiful all woven into a tapestry that will one day be extraordinary to behold.

An old acquaintance recently asked Keilah whether she wished she'd chosen differently regarding her pregnancy. Keilah responded, "I'm chasing my dreams with my daughter on my hip. She is not a burden, and I will never let a single seed of doubt be planted in her heart as to the validity of her life. She is not a mistake. She is loved. She is valuable. She is beautiful. And she is worthy of life. If I had to relive it all again just to have her, it would be worth it."

By all accounts Keilah was a victim, but she refused to live that way. So often hurt people hurt other people, and victims victimize others. However, she made a choice to break the chain that could have bound her. The bad choices made by her parents and by Brian would not define her or her daughter. Keilah has the final word in her story, and it's this: "I choose life, not fear."

———————

We can learn something powerful from Keilah: Choosing life is brave. Keilah is brave.

Every woman who faces the realities of an unplanned pregnancy and chooses life despite her circumstances is, quite simply and truly, a hero.

Chapter 4

External Pressure

The Effects of Providers, Partners, and
Parents on the Decision for Life

When Alaina's mom found out her daughter was pregnant, she immediately scheduled an abortion.

"If you want to stay in this home, get the abortion. You can't live here with a baby," her mom said.

Alaina knew her mom's threat was real; her sister had been kicked out the year before when she chose life for her baby.

Alaina erupted with emotions, pleading in tears for her mother to give her some time to think it over. She didn't want an abortion, but she was seventeen and in her senior year of high school. How could she maintain the stability she needed to graduate without family support? She was torn and didn't know where to turn. She reluctantly agreed to the appointment at the abortion clinic, but she couldn't shake the feeling that it wasn't the right thing to do.

On the day of her appointment, Alaina listened to her gut instinct and decided to make a different plan. She remembered that there was often a bus parked by her high school. It was a brightly colored mobile medical unit (MMU) that always caught her eye. The outside of the bus advertised free pregnancy tests and ultrasounds. She wondered, not very hopefully, if anyone had a better option for her.

In a last-second decision, Alaina pulled into a parking spot near the MMU. She took a deep breath, got out of her car, and walked toward it. Alaina received a warm welcome as she stepped on board. "I was supposed to get an abortion today, but I didn't go," she told Nicole, the nurse on duty. "I'm still just trying to figure this all out."

Seeing the uncertainty, fear, and confusion in Alaina's eyes, Nicole sat down with her and outlined her options. Using the booklet *Before You Decide*, Nicole worked through the pros and cons of parenting, adoption, and abortion, and they discussed how her choices would impact her life. Nicole gave Alaina a medically accurate description of the abortion procedure as well as key questions to ask the abortion clinic if she eventually chose to go there.

"Abortion is a medical procedure, and we want to make sure you know the potential risks and consequences associated with it," Nicole explained. "This full disclosure is expected with any other medical procedure, and you deserve to know exactly what you're choosing and what side effects could occur based on your choice."

Alaina leaned back in her seat and let out a sigh. For the first time since finding out she was pregnant, she was hearing facts and felt real freedom to choose instead of pressure to conform. Alaina felt hopeful and empowered after learning about all her options, especially the alternatives to abortion.

"I'm probably leaning more toward keeping the baby, but there is just a lot I have to figure out," she said.

"We will be here for you no matter what," Nicole reassured her with a smile. "I know it's a lot, but you will never be alone. Our team at the pregnancy center is here to help."

The center's social worker compiled community resources and referral numbers for her. Alaina left the bus with a packet of information to aid her in making her decision.

But her life continued to be more complicated than she wished. As much as she ached to keep her child, Alaina found herself sitting silently in an abortion clinic only two days after her encounter with Nicole.

"Alaina ... Alaina? ... Is there an Alaina in the room?"

A nurse appeared in the waiting room every few minutes and repeatedly called her name. But Alaina couldn't make herself respond and continued to sit quietly. Three hours went by. Her name was called a few more times, but she never answered. Finally, the nurse who had been calling her name approached her.

"You seem hesitant about having an abortion," she said. "If you're not sure this is what you want, you shouldn't do this."

Alaina had been drifting between two realities. She felt the full weight of losing her choice and her child, but in one moment, the words of the nurse pulled her back into her right mind. She realized that it really was her choice and she was strong enough to choose life.

> Not every woman feels safe and empowered to make her own choice about her pregnancy.

"Thank you," she told the nurse as she hurriedly gathered her things and darted out of the clinic.

As she slowly drove toward home, her foot rested lightly on the pedal and her hands held weakly to the steering wheel. Alaina observed everything around her that usually seemed ordinary. She wanted to soak it in as her thoughts raced. She still felt burdened with uncertainty and realized that this could be her last time going home. When Alaina avoided the first appointment, her mom set another one and forced her to go. By choosing her child, she would likely be kicked out of her parents' home at age seventeen and find herself pregnant, homeless, and unemployed.

Can I actually do this? she wondered. So many doubts flooded her heart and mind.

After she pulled into her driveway, Alaina sat inside her car with her eyes closed and her head down, breathing slowly to gain her composure. The conversation with her mother wouldn't be an easy one. Alaina held on to a thread of hope that her mom might be willing to care about her daughter and grandchild. She walked into the house and sat down with her mother, then told her that she planned to keep her baby. Instead of showing compassion, her mother lost control and screamed in rage at Alaina.

"How can you do this to me?" her mom shouted. "You're a disgrace, and I won't let you stay here if you're going to ruin your life. You have to be out of this house tonight!"

Alaina's heart was shattered. She had never imagined that she would someday face choosing between her mother and being a mother herself.

Pressure or Encouragement?

Alaina's story highlights the pivotal role that close friends, family, or partners play in a decision between abortion, adoption, and parenting. Not every woman feels safe and empowered to make her own choice about her pregnancy.

A study from the *Journal of American Physicians and Surgeons* found that almost three-quarters (73.8 percent) of women who had an abortion admitted feeling pressured to end their pregnancy. Of the 987 women who participated in the study, more than half said they chose abortion to make others happy, and 28.4 percent of respondents said they were afraid they would lose their partner if they didn't have an abortion.[1]

> "These findings are alarming," says Population Research Institute president Steven Mosher. "They suggest that a substantial number of women in America today who supposedly 'choose' abortion are

actually being pressured into it by their husbands, boyfriends, or family members.

"If a man tells a woman in so many words that he will leave her if she does not get an abortion, that woman is being denied the right to freely choose her—and her unborn child's—fate. The threat of abandonment is a very strong inducement to the woman not to carry her child to term."[2]

The Elliot Institute saw similar statistics. Their study *Forced Abortion in America* found that 64 percent of women reported feeling pressure to abort.[3]

In fact, there are multiple forms of pressure that those close to a woman may wield. Pressure can be subtle, such as suggesting the withdrawal of financial support or a partner threatening to leave. But there are more overt and dangerous forms of pressure, such as domestic violence or loss of housing.

The three major sources of pressure often exerted on women are parents, partners, or a prenatal diagnosis.

Prenatal Testing

Advancements in prenatal testing since the 1960s have enabled doctors to diagnose babies in utero and save lives. The ability to diagnose potential genetic diseases also allows parents to be informed and prepared before their baby arrives.

In the early 2000s, a new blood test became available that allowed easier screening for minor issues and birth defects. This test can be administered as early as ten to fourteen weeks into the pregnancy.

But the rise in testing and early detection has unintentionally caused a rise in abortion.

Across Europe, the abortion rate for babies with a detected genetic disease has skyrocketed over the years. In Denmark, 98 percent of pregnancies with a Down syndrome diagnosis are terminated; in Germany, it's 90 percent.[4]

Iceland has the highest abortion rate of any country in the world; nearly 100 percent of babies with a Down syndrome diagnosis are aborted. Geneticist Kári Stefánsson studies Iceland's genomes. He told CBS News that "we have basically eradicated ... Down syndrome from our society.... There is hardly ever a child with Down syndrome in Iceland anymore."[5]

While the abortion rate for a Down syndrome diagnosis in the United States isn't nearly that high, it is still well over half: 67 percent.[6]

For parents, wrestling with a chromosomal disorder or other adverse diagnoses isn't easy. Often, they are told by doctors that their child's quality of life will suffer if they choose life.

Christian singer/songwriter Matt Hammitt and his wife, Sarah, experienced this firsthand. They found out at their nineteen-week ultrasound that their son had a serious heart defect—hypoplastic left heart syndrome (HLHS). This abnormality of the baby's heart formation in the womb affects blood flow through the heart. HLHS is a type of congenital, or inherited, heart defect.

"The doctors told Sarah and me that the right and kind thing would be to 'terminate' our third pregnancy," Hammitt said. "They said our boy would be a burden to our family."

According to Project Heart, congenital heart disease (CHD) is the world's most common birth defect, affecting roughly forty thousand babies born in the United States each year. That means one in one hundred children in the US is born with CHD.[7]

There is very little data on the abortion rate of those with fetal anomalies like CHD. But in a 2004 study, the pro-choice Guttmacher

Institute found that about 13 percent of women chose abortion because of "possible problems affecting the health of the fetus."[8]

Another, from *The Journal of Maternal-Fetal & Neonatal Medicine*, studied 40,885 pregnancies to evaluate the frequency of abortion due to CHD. They found that 49 percent of families decided to terminate the pregnancy.[9]

The Hammitts chose life for their son and, over the years, have documented the difficulties of CHD in blogs, interviews, and a full-length documentary. But they have never once regretted it. Hammitt writes of his son Bowen: "Turns out, he has been an indescribable joy to us, and God is using his broken heart to help make others whole."

Although Bowen's life may be difficult at times, he is thriving and blessing those around him. His story also shows that a diagnosis doesn't mean a life of suffering. CDC statistics show that 95 percent of children born with noncritical CHDs survive to adulthood and 69 percent of children born with complex CHD survive to adulthood.[10] Additionally, survival rates have increased by almost 30 percent in the last ten years due to continued research and new treatments.[11]

The Hammitts are an example of beating the odds.

Pressure from Partners

Intimate partners hold an even stronger sway over women and their pregnancy decisions than doctors do. In fact, a Care Net study found that four in ten women who'd had abortions said the father of their child was the leading voice impacting their decision to abort.[12]

Having a supportive spouse or partner can make a huge difference in a choice for life. But a father who is opposed to a pregnancy can coerce a woman into an abortion when she may not want one.

The Guttmacher Institute released a study in 2005 called *Reasons U.S. Women Have Abortions: Quantitative and Qualitative Perspectives*. According to the study, 48 percent of women had an abortion because of relationship problems or apprehension about being a single mother.[13]

Partner-pressured abortions may also occur when a woman doesn't feel safe. As we've seen, violence in the home often escalates with pregnancy.

Pressure from Parents

Not only does the pressure to abort come from partners or doctors, though; it can also be expressed by friends and parents, especially the parents of dependent minors, like Alaina. Her story is a common example of how much pressure parents can wield, especially since minors typically rely on their parents or legal guardians for housing and finances.

Currently in the United States, thirty-seven states require parental consent for a minor to have an abortion. But what if the minor doesn't want an abortion and her parents still want her to go through with it? This is where things get murky.

From a legal standpoint, parents cannot force their teen to have an abortion. But they often use more subtle forms of pressure such as the threat of withholding support in the form of housing, income, or school enrollment.

The Justice Foundation, a nonprofit legal action organization, founded the Center Against Forced Abortions (CAFA). CAFA provides legal resources to minor mothers who feel they are being coerced into an abortion. The resources they offer include letters a woman can give to her parents or a doctor scheduled to perform an abortion. The letters provide language around the rights a woman possesses in making decisions for her child.

CAFA's parent letter from a minor states that the mother has the right to "direct the upbringing and education of her child.... That right is hers—not anyone else's. Although you still have the legal duty to care for her, protect, and provide for her, she has the right to make decisions to keep the child in her womb, your grandchild."

The letter also notes that a minor's rights to keep her baby are upheld by the United States Supreme Court:

> Even though abortion may be legal, you do not have any right to *force, coerce, exert undue influence or unduly pressure* your daughter to have an abortion. The United States Supreme Court makes it clear that an abortion decision by a minor must be hers, that it must be free, voluntary, and non-coerced. See *Bellotti v. Baird*, 443 U.S. 622 (1979). Force, excessive coercion, or duress may also subject you to reporting and prosecution for child abuse.[14]

The foundation also created a letter that a woman can give or send to an abortion provider in the event she is taken there for an abortion against her wishes. The letter states:

> I am currently pregnant and I am aware that state and federal law allows me to obtain the reproductive health care which I determine to be in my best interest, including abortion or prenatal care. After having fully considered all of my options, I have independently decided to continue my pregnancy to

> term. However, I am being subjected to coercion by
> others which is meant to compel me to terminate
> my pregnancy.... Should you perform an abortion
> on me despite being informed of this fact, you
> may be subject to criminal prosecution and/or civil
> liability.[15]

Sarah Jansen, a licensed clinical social worker at a pregnancy center, said minors often come to their clinic looking for help in this area. They provide the letters from CAFA to help them understand and voice their legal rights as minors.

When minors get pregnant and don't know how to navigate all the implications of suddenly being an independent adult, PRCs step in to help. They connect pregnant or parenting minors to supportive resources like maternity homes; the Women, Infants, and Children (WIC) office for Medicaid; and other resource-based programs.

In Alaina's case, the pregnancy center helped her navigate everything.

Alaina's Story Continued

After the extremely negative response from her mother, the reality of Alaina's situation sank in. Feeling that she had nowhere else to turn, Alaina went back to the pregnancy center's bus. Both the nurse and the social worker she had met on her first visit sat down with her. Together they worked to create a chart for and against both abortion and parenting, weighing the pros and cons for each option. They also discussed ways the pregnancy center could help if Alaina truly was unable to stay at her mom's house. Everything was written down to help Alaina clearly see all her concerns, thoughts, and feelings.

After creating an extensive list, Nicole asked Alaina what was most important to her on the list of pros and cons. Taking the pen and crossing out everything that didn't matter, Alaina finally circled "I love my baby."

At that moment, the atmosphere around them shifted. Everyone realized that Alaina's heart was set on securing the safety of her child, no matter what circumstances she might face as a result of her decision. It no longer mattered that she had been kicked out of her home; she knew her friends at the pregnancy center would be family to her and would help her through anything. Knowing she would not be alone in the journey, Alaina resolved to choose life.

The staff at the pregnancy center connected Alaina to a local nonprofit designed to help mothers for up to five years, beginning with their pregnancy. They would walk with Alaina as she found a doctor, acquired insurance, and secured government aid for housing, food bills, and college tuition.

A local church jumped in to support Alaina's needs for childcare, community, mentoring, and household furnishing. Alaina joined the pregnancy center's Earn While You Learn program that provided the diapers, clothing, and other supplies she would need in the early years of her child's life.

> Taking the pen and crossing out everything that didn't matter, Alaina finally circled "I love my baby."

From her journey, Alaina learned that true choice existed when all the facts combined with the space to think through her fears, dreams, and concerns. She realized that abortion became an option only because others thought she couldn't or shouldn't become a mother. She showed her strength in not allowing circumstances or others to pressure her into doing what she didn't actually want to do. The local pregnancy center's support and their abundant resources helped her realize her own strength.

She chose life because she loved her baby, and no one could force her to change that. By being given the right to choose, Alaina experienced empowerment.

Wondering Where to Start?

You and your church have the opportunity to start brainstorming ways to provide housing for minors who might suddenly become homeless because of an unplanned pregnancy. Find people in your congregation who have spare bedrooms, apartments, or rental properties that might be available for emergency housing.

Start a fund in your budget for your local pregnancy resource center to use for the needs of young mothers. You could organize a drive at your church to collect necessary items—diapers, baby supplies, and maternity clothing—for your local PRC or maternity home.

If there are maternity homes in your area, connect with one and volunteer. Or encourage individuals in your congregation with counseling backgrounds to spend time mentoring young women at a local maternity home or pregnancy center.

Additionally, have copies of the Justice Foundation's letters on hand at your church.

Reflecting the Father's Heart

Countless times Scripture reveals God caring for the lives of the weak and vulnerable. The first example of a single mom appears in Genesis 16. Hagar, the Egyptian slave of Abraham and Sarah, became pregnant with Abraham's son Ishmael, but Sarah mistreated her and forced her away from her home. The angel of the Lord comforted

Hagar and offered her hope, protection, and promises. When she recognized that God saw her suffering, she reacted with gratitude, saying, "'You are the God who sees me,' for she said, 'I have now seen the One who sees me'" (v. 13).

God's heart to care for those who are hurting, oppressed, facing difficult times, ostracized, or struggling in life never changes.

> He has shown you, O mortal, what is good.
>   And what does the LORD require of you?
> To act justly and to love mercy
>   and to walk humbly with your God. (Mic. 6:8)

Seeking justice and loving mercy require humility. We must humble our own hearts to listen to what God says about human life and how He calls us to serve others. There are many expressions of being merciful and seeking justice for women like Alaina, and we must do them all in love.

Prayer

Father, show me how to love those facing unplanned pregnancies as You do. Help me understand the sometimes-complicated issues associated with a pro-life perspective, and inspire me to make a godly difference. Empower me and Your church to positively impact the lives of women, men, and children around the world. I invite You to shape my heart to be more like Yours. Make me sensitive to the needs of those in my community. Thank You for the life You've given me; help me use my life to love and serve others well. Amen.

Chapter 5

Domestic Abuse

How Abuse Affects Pregnancy Decisions and Why the Church Must Act

"If it's not okay to talk about, it's not okay for people to get help."

Victoria Thomas, LPC, MA

Jacqueline's twenty-first birthday was quite the bash. She and her friends celebrated hard that night, which is partly why she doesn't remember all that much. Especially how she got the bruise on her arm.

It ached all the next day through the haze of her hangover, but she reasoned she had probably fallen into something when she was drunk. She asked her boyfriend, Keith, if he remembered how she had hurt her arm, but he didn't offer many details.

Moving in with Keith had seemed like a good idea just a few months ago. She wanted to forget about the fragmentation of her family, the violence between her parents, and the constant depression she found herself in. Keith made her feel seen, at least some of the time. But lately things had been escalating, and he was getting angry at her more and more often.

The neighbors called the police more than once to investigate the excessive noise coming from their house. But Jacqueline always felt the need to protect Keith rather than protecting herself when the police showed up. She didn't feel like she deserved much anyway; she was just happy to be noticed occasionally.

Jacqueline didn't realize at the time that she was a victim of domestic violence and psychological abuse. She wanted to help Keith become the better man he always said he could be. Jacqueline was caught up in patterns that had been going on for years.

Her story is not uncommon. Domestic abuse happens every day all around the world. The National Coalition Against Domestic Violence (NCADV) defines domestic violence this way:

> [It] is the willful intimidation, physical assault, battery, sexual assault, and/or other abusive behavior as part of a systematic pattern of power and control perpetrated by one intimate partner against another. It includes physical violence, sexual violence, psychological violence, and emotional abuse.[1]

These patterns are part of what makes abuse so complicated and multilayered.

Jacqueline's story became more complex when, one night, all hell broke loose. She can't remember what they were fighting about, but their screaming match escalated quickly. Jacqueline felt adrenaline pulse through her veins as she narrowly escaped the bowl whirling toward her head. Dodging that dish cost her as she smashed her face into the edge of the counter. A few more dishes flew her direction, some hitting the target, others hitting the wall.

This time when the police showed up, they saw her black eye and the shattered glass and asked her if they could get her out of the house. She agreed and sought refuge with a friend for a few days. That is, until Keith called her, apologizing profusely. He vowed to be a better man and that he would never hurt her again. Against her friend's advice, she decided to move back in with him. Deep down she loved Keith and wanted to believe him, so she decided to give him another chance.

Nausea overwhelmed Jacqueline shortly after moving back in with Keith. A shiver of fear stronger than any she'd felt when facing his anger froze her heart.

Could I be pregnant? she wondered.

> # Women facing abusive partners may choose abortion as an act of self-preservation.

If she was, she knew she couldn't bring a baby into her current situation. After searching "how do I know if I'm pregnant," Jacqueline found the number to a nearby pregnancy center that offered free pregnancy tests and ultrasounds. She figured abortion would be the best decision for her, considering her circumstances, but without much extra money and not wanting Keith to know, the opportunity to get a free pregnancy test and ultrasound was too good to pass up.

During the intake process, the pregnancy center staff asked Jacqueline about her story. She usually didn't say much about her past or even present circumstances to anyone. Talking about the fights that had resulted in her bruises was not something she wanted to do, yet the women facilitating the intake process made her feel safe enough to tell the truth.

After relating part of the journey that had brought her there, Jacqueline lay down on the exam table for the ultrasound. The flat screen on the wall came to life and displayed the little head and body of her ten-week-old baby. The baby appeared to wiggle, and a smile crossed Jacqueline's face for the first time in a while. But then her countenance shifted as she began to think of Keith's reaction. She didn't feel safe.

Domestic Violence and Abuse

In the United States alone, an average of twenty people experience domestic violence every minute.

Domestic abuse includes physical violence, sexual violence, psychological harm, and stalking by a current or former partner or spouse.

The NCADV reports that, on a typical day, domestic violence hotlines nationwide receive more than twenty thousand calls. The coalition also reports that one in four women (24.3 percent) and one in seven men (13.8 percent) aged eighteen and older in the United States have been the victims of severe physical violence by an intimate partner.[2]

Chances are you know someone who has been abused or is currently being abused. Jacqueline's experience occurs in our communities and our neighborhoods, often right under our noses.

Domestic Violence and Pregnancy

Ultimately, domestic violence is about control. It is a pattern of behavior by one individual in an intimate relationship in order to exert and maintain power over the other person. For women facing a violent partner, an unplanned pregnancy on top of abuse can feel like a life sentence.

The Guttmacher Institute, a pro-choice research group, studied situations in which men threatened to hurt their partners in order to end the pregnancies. It found that women facing abusive partners may choose abortion as an act of self-preservation.

In one interview they conducted, a twenty-one-year-old respondent said her partner threatened to harm her and her unborn child:

> Respondent: He sat there and was like, "If you don't get it done, I'm throwing you down the steps, or I'm doing something!"

Interviewer: Did that scare you?

Respondent: … Yeah, because I probably could believe he would do it.… One time, he was like, "I'll just punch in your stomach," and I am thinking, *Oh yeah, he punched me on my face; he might punch me in my stomach.…* Feeling the baby there, it was, like, *I can't do this.… This is crazy.* I was like, "If it doesn't get done [by a doctor], he's going to do it, and I don't want that to be done. So if it's going to be done, it's going to be done [the] right way."[3]

Why It's So Hard to Leave

From the outside looking in, it may seem obvious to think that a woman could just leave her abusive partner. Those who have never experienced abuse believe it's mainly physical, but domestic abuse is much more complicated than that. Mental and emotional components create a further bond in the relationship that is hard to break.

According to the National Domestic Violence Hotline (NDVH), domestic violence behaviors are typically ones that physically harm, incite fear, prevent a partner from doing what he or she wants, or force a partner to do things he or she does not want to do. This includes:

Intimidation: making her afraid by using looks, actions, or gestures (smashing or breaking things, displaying weapons).

Isolation: controlling what she does, whom she sees and talks to, what she reads, or where she goes.

Economic abuse: preventing her from getting or keeping a job or making her ask for money.

Emotional abuse: making her feel bad about herself, calling her names, or making her think she's crazy.[4]

Often abuse manifests itself as one or all of the behaviors listed above. These manipulative relationships are full of psychological minefields. Jacqueline's story highlights the complicated and tragic nature of abusive relationships. The truth is, humans are hardwired for connection and have a deep longing to be loved and cared for. In cases of domestic abuse, the concept of love is twisted and relationship dynamics become horribly broken.

"There is an emotional dependence piece to abusive relationships," explained Victoria Thomas, a licensed professional counselor who has spent the last ten years of her career working with victims of abuse and trauma.

"With victims," she said, "it's a lot about how they view themselves. They often don't believe they deserve better. Their lives are so intertwined with the abuser. They become dependent on a person for their needs to be met."

Violence in the home can also intensify after news of a pregnancy. The American College of Obstetricians and Gynecologists (ACOG) reports that approximately 324,000 pregnant women are abused each year in the United States.[5] Violence or the fear of violence causes some women to choose an abortion who otherwise might not.

In the Guttmacher study *Reasons U.S. Women Have Abortions: Quantitative and Qualitative Perspectives*, 14 percent of women reported that their husbands or partners explicitly wanted them to get an abortion.[6] This form of pressure is known as reproductive coercion, defined by the ACOG as follows:

> Reproductive and sexual coercion involves behavior intended to maintain power and control in a relationship related to reproductive health by someone who is, was, or wishes to be involved in an intimate or dating relationship with an adult or adolescent. This behavior includes explicit attempts to impregnate a partner against her will, control outcomes of a pregnancy, coerce a partner to have unprotected sex, and interfere with contraceptive methods.[7]

An article from the peer-reviewed journal *PLOS Medicine* says that reproductive coercion also includes forcing a female partner to terminate a pregnancy when she does not want to or injuring a female partner in a way that may cause a miscarriage.[8]

Intimate partner violence (IPV) (another term for domestic violence) is so common that the ACOG recommends screening for violence "at the first prenatal visit, at least once per trimester, and at the postpartum checkup."[9]

In fact, pregnancy often heightens the risk of being attacked, increasing rates of homicide as a result. A 2020 study from *JAMA Pediatrics* found that homicide is a leading cause of death among pregnant and postpartum women in Louisiana. Of the 119 pregnancy-associated deaths in the state in 2016 and 2017, 13.4 percent (16) were homicides. The researchers estimated that for every one hundred thousand women who were pregnant or postpartum, there were 12.9 homicide deaths, which outnumbered deaths from any single obstetric cause, including hypertensive disorders (3.2) and amniotic fluid entering the bloodstream (4.8). The risk of homicide death was twice as high for women and girls during pregnancy and the postpartum period, compared with women and girls who were not pregnant or postpartum.[10]

How can this violence be stopped if victims are isolated, fearful, or psychologically manipulated?

Providing Safety

If an abused woman is going to choose life, the immediate role of a pregnancy center is to help her feel safe while acknowledging that her fears of raising a child in an abusive home are valid. No mother wants to bring a child into the world only to join in her suffering. Instead, she has to know there is a safe place for her to go where her abuser cannot find her and continue to harm her.

Leaving an abusive relationship requires time and careful planning; a woman needs to develop and implement a safety plan. The NDVH describes a safety plan as "a personalized, practical plan to improve your safety while experiencing abuse, preparing to leave an abusive situation, or after you leave."[11] Safety planning involves how to cope with emotions, how to tell friends and family about the abuse, how to take legal action, and more. Pregnancy resource centers that discover a violent domestic situation can walk a client through the process of developing a safety plan.

The NDVH helps women create personalized safety plans, including a strategy for leaving and what they will need: identification, legal papers, emergency numbers, a possible police escort, a new cell phone, and more. On their website, the organization specifically recommends the following to women preparing to leave a relationship:

- Keep any evidence of physical abuse, such as pictures of injuries.
- Maintain a journal of all violent incidents, noting dates, events, and threats made, if possible. Keep your journal in a safe place.

- Know where you can go to get help. Tell someone what is happening.
- Plan with your children, and identify a safe place for them to go in an emergency, like a room with a lock or a friend's house where they would likely find help. Reassure them that their job is to stay safe, not to protect you. [12]

Economic abuse and inadequate access to housing are some of the leading reasons that women find it so difficult to exit an abusive relationship, but pregnancy centers are equipped to help. The US Department of Health and Human Services' Office on Women's Health has state-specific lists of programs and resources. PRC staff members can assist women with finding alternative housing or connect them to safe houses through these lists and with resources they've curated in their own communities. Most states also have organizations like TESSA, which provides safe housing for women fleeing domestic violence.

In a time of crisis, often what's needed most is someone outside the situation to provide perspective and guidance about the next steps.

Your Church Can Make a Difference

The local church can be an important ally on this issue.

"The churches I have seen handle this issue well are those that are connected with mental health professionals," Victoria Thomas said. "A church that's willing to wrestle with the question of how to tackle domestic abuse is a church that's equipped to learn how to handle it."

This is a unique opportunity for churches to partner with mental health professionals in their communities.

"The best thing you can do for a woman in an abusive relationship is encourage her to seek a therapist," Thomas noted. "That way when she's ready to leave, people can step in and help. Most therapists are qualified to handle this in a way that's discreet."

If a woman is worried about the cost or unsure where to find a therapist, she has options. She can call the NDVH, and they will direct her to resources in her community. Local women's shelters and safe houses can also provide referrals to counseling and legal organizations that might offer pro bono work. The Substance Abuse and Mental Health Services Administration has a Behavioral Health Treatment Services Locator, where you can search for therapy. They also have payment assistance and sliding-scale fee options you can choose as you search. While there is no one-size-fits-all solution, most local and national organizations have a robust referral list that can quickly connect a woman to a safe place or to someone who can support her as she seeks refuge.

Churches willing to connect with community organizations that provide safe housing, offer counseling, or work directly with victims are better able to discern where they can help tackle the problem of abuse in their neighborhoods. "The church has to be in a position to say, 'We are not aware of what needs to happen. Help us understand what is needed. Educate us so we can help,'" Thomas suggested.

Jacqueline's Story Continued

The PRC staff listened to Jacqueline's story with concern and compassion and reinforced their commitment to support her. Once they understood Jacqueline's pain and current financial situation, the pregnancy center nurses offered numerous supportive services. They helped Jacqueline develop a safety plan, and she located a temporary safe home until her application for government housing aid was approved. She learned about the organizations in her community that were ready to help her find stability. Within this new community of supportive people was a therapist who helped her heal from her abusive relationship.

Jacqueline stayed connected to the staff, who befriended her and helped her see the possibility of choosing life for her child. Through the months leading up to her delivery, the pregnancy center and her local church supported Jacqueline emotionally and physically. She joined classes and continued her therapy. She and her son began a new life together with the continued encouragement of her local pregnancy center and support groups. Once she was physically safe, Jacqueline was at peace again and able to receive the message of her God-given value.

Wondering Where to Start?

Research the organizations in your community that serve and support women seeking safety from domestic violence. Ask them about ways you could partner to serve and support those seeking safety.

Visit the Office on Women's Health (www.womenshealth.gov) to access the state resources available to women facing abuse. Your church can keep these on hand as a reference.

Determine whether your community has organizations that provide safe housing, like TESSA. Ask how your church can get involved in their initiatives.

Educate yourself on domestic abuse through the NDVH website (www.thehotline.org). The better you understand their wealth of information on the issue, the more easily you will be able to share it with your friends or church family.

Contact your local women's shelter to find out about laws and available resources they offer for women looking to leave an abusive relationship. WomensLaw.org lists state-by-state legal information.

> As Christ's body operating in a broken world, we are called to point people to His truth and fight the lies that attempt to destroy God's treasured creation.

Then become the catalyst in your church body to bring awareness of the issue of domestic abuse and how it specifically relates to women facing pregnancy. Contact your local county social services to ask if they offer mandated reporter trainings. After key people in your church attend the training, talk about this issue in small groups and determine how your church can support hurting women in your neighborhood.

If you're still not sure where to start, locate your local PRC and ask them how they assist pregnant women in abusive situations. If you feel passionate about this, pray for the opportunity to bring God's hope and healing to those at risk near you. Search Save the Storks' national pro-life index at www.savethestorks.com to find organizations near you.

Reflecting the Father's Heart

Speak up for those who cannot speak for themselves,
for the rights of all who are destitute.
Speak up and judge fairly;
defend the rights of the poor and needy.
(Prov. 31:8–9)

As Christ's body operating in a broken world, we are called to point people to His truth and fight the lies that attempt to destroy God's treasured creation. Violence against humanity is wrong and heartbreaking no matter when, where, or to whom it happens. The violence perpetrated against a woman by those who should protect her compounds the devastating tragedy of abortion.

Imagine the power for change in our communities, in our country, and in the lives of families if just one person from every church committed to help one individual find safety and healing from domestic abuse. Picture the eternal impact of one person helping a woman in an unplanned pregnancy feel equipped to choose life for herself and her child.

Prayer

Father, help me to see, serve, and save those who are caught in domestic abuse right now. I ask that You fill my mouth with Your words to speak for those who do not have a voice or are too afraid to speak up. Use me to raise awareness of the issues that break Your heart. Your Son experienced every kind of violence and abuse, so You know the pain people feel when those who are family or those who should care turn against them. God, help those suffering in abusive situations right now. Make a way for them to connect with someone, even me, to find safety and, ultimately, salvation in You. Thank You for the healing You offer to every one of us who is broken. Show me how to bring Your love and healing to those around me. In Jesus' name I ask this. Amen.

Chapter 6

Sexual Violence and Rape

"Creating a second victim never undoes the damage to the first."

Randy Alcorn, *Why Pro-Life?*

"My birth mom's courage enabled me to exist, to get married, and to have four incredible kids. She went through incredible pain, but she chose to be stronger than her circumstances."

Ryan Bomberger, founder of the Radiance Foundation

"I can't have this baby," Shey said.

Her words mixed with heavy sobs were nearly impossible to discern on the pregnancy resource center's voice mail. Shey had just taken a pregnancy test, and she was devastated. Her pregnancy was a result of rape.

Debbie, the executive director of the pregnancy center, was in the habit of checking the center's voice mails over weekends just in case there was an emergency call. Debbie knew right away: this was urgent. She called Shey back immediately.

The shame and trauma choked Shey's words as she told Debbie what had happened. This wasn't Shey's first time being raped.

"Why does this keep happening to me?" she asked.

"This is not your fault," Debbie reassured her. "I know it's hard not to believe the lie that it *is* your fault, but the truth is, someone forced himself on you. It feels so wrong because he took your choice from you."

Shey couldn't imagine having this baby, but she remembered the words her mom had told her years ago.

"Whatever you do in life, do not get an abortion," her mom cautioned, speaking from the pain of her own experience.

Through the conversation, Shey was reassured of her value and the support Debbie's PRC would provide to her. With two other children at home, Shey really didn't feel capable of parenting this child, but she had a friend who offered to adopt her baby.

Debbie invited both Shey and her friend to the pregnancy center to ensure that Shey truly understood her options and the difference between an open and closed adoption. Together they began working on a plan with a local agency to facilitate an open adoption for Shey's baby.

Though the child was conceived in trauma, his life would not have to be filled with it.

Addressing Rape

It's hard enough to process the emotional and physical trauma of rape. It's even harder when a raped woman becomes pregnant.

Because rape is one of the most difficult issues, in general, for women to talk about, it's also one of the most complex issues to address when it comes to the pro-life movement.

Rape is a form of sexual assault (although not all sexual assault is rape). It is nonconsensual sexual contact or intercourse that sometimes results in pregnancy.

Although rape is not the most common reason cited for unplanned pregnancies, it is often used by pro-choice advocates to argue for unrestricted abortion in the United States. And this is why the pro-life side needs to be able to speak on this issue with compassion and understanding. Even as we value the life of the baby, it's crucial to acknowledge the immense trauma, fear, and pain that sexual assault inflicts.

Megan Almon works for Life Training Institute (https://pro-lifetraining.com), an organization that coaches people to effectively make the case for life. She speaks to students all across the country on abortion, including the issue of rape.

"We [as the pro-life community] have to walk into this issue with eyes wide open," she said. "This is a hard issue. We have to approach with love and compassion women who have been victims of rape."

The Truth in Numbers

"Approximately eighteen million women have experienced vaginal rape at some point in their life."[1]

RAINN (Rape, Abuse & Incest National Network, www.rainn.org) is the nation's largest anti–sexual violence organization. They run the National Sexual Assault Hotline as well as programs to help prevent sexual violence. Their statistics on women and sexual assault are staggering:

- On average, there are 463,634 victims (age 12 or older) of rape and sexual assault each year in the United States.
- 82% of all juvenile [rape] victims are female.
- 90% of adult rape victims are female.
- Females ages 16–19 are four times more likely than the general population to be victims of rape, attempted rape, or sexual assault.
- Women ages 18–24 who are college students are three times more likely than women in general to experience sexual violence. Females of the same age who are not enrolled in college are four times more likely.
- One out of every six American women has been the victim of an attempted or completed rape in her lifetime.[2]

Think about that last stat for a moment. One out of every six.

And after the assault, there are often years of trauma and emotional fallout.

"It is the epitome of evil," said Almon regarding sexual assault. "It is all about taking, with no consideration of the victim's humanity or immeasurable worth."

Perhaps the best way to grow a perspective of compassion is by attempting to understand the trauma of rape through a survivor's account.

Jennifer's Story

Jennifer Christie was a devoted wife and mother of four who enjoyed her work as a sign-language interpreter. Her job often required her to travel away from her family. In January 2014, her two-week out-of-town work assignment required staying in a hotel. On the last day of the trip, a snowstorm rolled into town, causing her event to end early. She braved the cold, trudging back to her room through the snow, scarf wrapped around her neck and head. The wind made it difficult to hear anything around her.

"I walked up to my room and didn't know I was being followed," she said.

Jennifer felt relieved when she made it to her door. She pulled off her gloves and fumbled to get her key from her purse, then opened the door and walked inside her warm, quiet room to set her things down on the desk. She turned around to see a man she didn't recognize standing silently in the doorway.

"He gave me a strange smile, and then he punched me in the head," she said.

It's painful for Jennifer to recall details from that day, but being violently hit is one of the last things she can clearly remember from those life-altering moments. She struggled to escape, but she couldn't get free from his grip. Depleted of her strength, her body finally gave in. After the blackout, she can't remember anything.

"I awoke to a woman screaming," Jennifer said. She remembers that other woman's screams so vividly. Though she was in a haze, she sensed how badly she was hurt by the responses of the people rushing in to help.

Jennifer was found lying in an outside stairwell, most of her clothes ripped from her body and her hands covered in blood. The hotel staff sprang into action to cover her and make her as comfortable as possible until the first responders could arrive. The ambulance rushed Jennifer to the hospital, where she was treated for fractured ribs, broken fingers, internal damage, and a brain bleed. Her emotional and physical trauma was horrifying, but it was just the beginning.

Jennifer's husband, Jeff, was committed to her recovery, helping her each step of the way. Their first priority was the physical healing from her assault. Each day was filled with its own challenges, but she made good progress with Jeff's support and the help of her doctors.

A few weeks later, Jennifer decided to go back to work. She and Jeff agreed it would be best to keep her mind busy and to actively move forward.

Her first assignment after the incident held promise of being more than a job. She was asked to sign on a cruise ship, which gave her an opportunity for rest and relaxation as well. A couple of days into the cruise, she started to feel frustrated because sea sickness was interrupting what was supposed to be a relaxing trip. After two days with no relief, the doctors on the ship decided to give her more aggressive treatment. But before prescribing a new regimen, one of the doctors asked her if there was any chance she could be pregnant.

"I stopped, and for the first time out loud, I said, 'I was raped.' It's just an ugly, ugly word. I had this feeling in my stomach, so I told him he might want to test me," she recounted.

The ship doctors handed Jennifer a pregnancy test and gave her a few minutes by herself. Away from home and alone at sea, she watched as two blue lines appeared in front of her. Jennifer was pregnant.

Frantic, she reached for her phone to call Jeff. She paused for a moment in uncertainty: unsure whether she would have service, unsure of how to say it, unsure of how he would respond. She was afraid, but Jeff had always been so supportive. She had to believe he would support her through this too. She found the courage to dial him, and Jeff picked up. Her words clumsily spilled out, and she waited through seconds of silence that felt like hours.

Finally Jeff spoke: "Sweetheart, this is a gift. This is something beautiful from something so painful and terrible. We can do this."

> Though the child was conceived in trauma,
> his life would not have to be filled with it.

"This was the darkest time in my life," Jennifer said. "But for the first time since the assault, I felt something come alive in me again. I felt hope and joy and light. I remember thinking I couldn't protect myself but I could protect that baby. It was *my* baby."

Jennifer recalls that she spent the next week with cruise ship doctors and nurses consoling her and letting her know how "easy" it would be to "take care of" the fetus. Against the advice of so many around her, months later she welcomed a son into the world.

"He is an integral part of the family," she said. "He's this bright spot. He's joy and laughter and silliness."

People often ask Jennifer where God was when she was assaulted and how she can believe in a God who would allow rape and violence in the world.

"My God was all over my story," she tells them. "I was being dragged away from the scene, and someone stepped in and prevented me from being carried off. The snow saved my brain from swelling. This child gave me a reason to want to press on."

What Do the Numbers Tell Us?

Jennifer continues to tell her story to this day because she wants to show other women that there is hope, even in such an atrocious and horrible situation. She says she wants the thirty-two thousand women who conceive because of rape every year to know they are not alone.

In fact, according to a study published by the *American Journal of Obstetrics and Gynecology*, 32.2 percent of women who conceive because of rape still decide to keep their children and 5.9 percent place their children for adoption, while 11.8 percent miscarry.[3]

The remaining 50 percent choose to have an abortion.

Yet, contrary to what women may expect, this perceived solution doesn't necessarily further their healing. An interesting study by the Elliot Institute, a pro-life advocacy group, found that, of women who had an abortion after rape, 80 percent reported that the abortion had been the wrong solution and most women reported that the abortion had only increased their trauma. The study was based on responses from 192 women who became pregnant from either rape or incest (164 were victims of rape, 28 of incest). None of the women who chose to give birth expressed regret for the child or wished they had aborted instead.[4]

Ryan's Story

Ryan Bomberger is the cofounder of the Radiance Foundation, a pro-life nonprofit that uses digital media and storytelling to affirm the beauty of life. He started the foundation because he was conceived in rape.

"I am the 1 percent that is used 100 percent of the time to justify abortion," he often shares in speeches.

According to the Guttmacher Institute, 1 percent of women choose to abort because the child was conceived in rape.[5]

Since his mother chose to carry him and place him for adoption, rape and abortion are topics that are close to Ryan's heart. "My birth mom experienced the horror and violence of rape but rejected the further violence of abortion. That's why I'm here today," he said. "I am alive today because of a courageous birth mom. She chose to be stronger than her circumstances…. My birth mom's singular decision will cause beautiful reverberations for generations." He grew up as one of thirteen children in a multiracial family, and today he has four children of his own, two of whom are adopted.

Ryan doesn't deny the fact that rape and abortion are hard to talk about. But he notes that our culture believes the only solution to rape is abortion. Through his work as a speaker, he talks to rape survivors all over the country, many of whom have had abortions.

"I hear from them that abortion is like a second rape," he said. "Here you have a woman who is violently violated; then a life is taken. That abortionist, like the rapist, leaves. And no one is there to deal with the aftermath of all that."

In talking to rape survivors who chose life for their babies, he says the common thread is that the child is the only redemptive part of such a violent act.

"The violence of abortion does not cure the violence of rape," Ryan said.

The Pro-Life Answer

If the research and stories show that women who have an abortion after rape feel even more trauma, how do we increase the dialogue about this as the pro-life community? How do we talk about post-rape pregnancy without shrinking back from what's right, even if it's asking people to do hard things? If we're not talking about it, how can we begin to help women deal with the trauma?

"This is really, really hard," said Megan Almon of Life Training Institute. "But here is what I know to be true: the unborn baby is unquestionably human from the moment of conception, and we can't kill innocent human beings because they might remind us of something terrible."

The reality is that abortion, the killing of an unborn child, is still wrong in these cases. Almon did note that in order to make that statement, we first have to acknowledge the emotional hardship a woman is facing. But if we as pro-life people believe that the unborn are tiny humans, then we have to make the case for life—even in the hard scenarios.

> My God was all over my story.... This child
> gave me a reason to want to press on.

"In a broken world, we find ourselves in a scenario where evil has been acted upon another," Almon said, summarizing ideas gleaned from Christopher Kaczor in his book *The Ethics of Abortion*. "The normal decision a woman would have, to decide to have a child, is taken from her. When a woman conceives because of rape, it is profoundly unfair. We have to acknowledge that. She did not want it or ask for it."

Because it is not something she was planning for, the church and pro-life organizations are needed to provide help and recovery. Life Training Institute provides numerous resources to aid the pro-life movement in addressing this subject and, most importantly, help women deal with the trauma they survived.

Counseling for Victims of Sexual Violence

Another vital resource for those who have experienced rape is Christian counseling. The American Association of Christian Counselors (AACC) is the largest organization of Christian counselors in the United States. One of their main initiatives is to create resources to help people find licensed counselors and faith-based treatment centers. Their search tool, Christian Care Connect (https://connect.aacc.net), connects clients with counselors and clinics so those in need of mental health services can locate someone in their area.

"A good counselor can help women navigate this situation. The most important thing is her health and the health of the baby. That includes medically, emotionally, and spiritually," said Dr. Tim Clinton, president of the AACC.

For Clinton, getting the church involved is key.

"Women are a sleeping giant in the church," he said. "But they are often silenced because they carry the shame or stigma of their past [whether it's rape or an abortion]. Yet so many of these women can step in and be a point of light. They can talk about their decision, and they can help educate, engage, and equip the church in this area."

And they can tell their stories. That's what makes Jennifer Christie's decision to raise her son such a powerful message for life.

She wrote the following on her blog:

During a nightmare I couldn't awake from, a child was conceived. This child had nothing to do with the attack on my body or the scars on my soul. He had everything to do with my healing—giving me a reason to hope. I did not save my son. He saved me.

I am not raising a "rapist's baby." I am raising my baby. He is the love that I pour into him. He is the love of my husband who is raising him and siblings who play with him and the grandparents who dote on him. He is all of these things and more. As unique as a fingerprint, he has something that is just him. And he's perfect.

Is he a reminder? He is. He's a reminder that, as women, we can be stronger than our circumstances. He's a reminder that beauty can come from darkness. And he's a reminder that how we began does not determine how we end.[6]

Wondering Where to Start?

Acquaint yourself with resources on the Life Training Institute website, or invite one of their members to hold a workshop in your church. You and your church can learn about the trauma of rape and how you can connect hurting women with resources to process their pain.

RAINN offers an array of services for churches and pregnancy resource centers to access. These include a 24-7 hotline that connects people with a RAINN support specialist or a local center from their network of more than a thousand sexual-assault service providers throughout the country. They also provide consulting, program assessments, and sexual assault awareness training. The training educates attendees and prepares them to support survivors of sexual assault and works well for a church or pregnancy resource center staff. Training includes modules like Sexual Assault 101, Understanding Trauma Responses, and Basics of Crisis Intervention.

Empower your church staff and leaders to know how to talk with survivors and train others. The following is some specific language that RAINN's National Sexual Assault Hotline staff recommends when talking with survivors and helping them with the healing process:

- *"I believe you. / It took a lot of courage to tell me about this."* Survivors can find it difficult to share what happened to them. They may feel ashamed or worried they won't be believed. The best thing you can do is support them.
- *"It's not your fault. / You didn't do anything to deserve this."* Survivors often blame themselves. It's important to remind them that they did nothing wrong.
- *"You are not alone. / I care about you and want to help in any way I can."* Let the survivor know that you are there to support her and listen. Help her find services, like therapy, that can assist her in her healing process.
- *"I'm sorry this happened. / This shouldn't have happened to you."* Acknowledge the survivor's trauma and pain. Communicate empathy with statements like *"This must be really tough for you"* and *"I'm so glad you are sharing this with me."*[7]

Reflecting the Father's Heart

The Spirit of the Sovereign LORD is on me,
    because the LORD has anointed me
    to proclaim good news to the poor.

He has sent me to bind up the brokenhearted,
>   to proclaim freedom for the captives
>   and release from darkness for the prisoners,
> to proclaim the year of the LORD's favor
>   and the day of vengeance of our God,
> to comfort all who mourn,
>   and provide for those who grieve in Zion—
> to bestow on them a crown of beauty
>   instead of ashes,
> the oil of joy
>   instead of mourning,
> and a garment of praise
>   instead of a spirit of despair.
> They will be called oaks of righteousness,
>   a planting of the LORD
>   for the display of his splendor. (Isa. 61:1–3)

God invites us to be part of His restorative work in the world. There is no shortage of brokenness and hearts that need healing. In Luke 4:21, Jesus announced that He was the fulfillment of God's promise to redeem humanity. He also told His disciples, "Whoever believes in me will do the works I have been doing, and they will do even greater things than these" (John 14:12).

If you have rape in your past, you may be the one needing to trade ashes for a crown and to see your mourning replaced by joy. Ask someone in your church about the counseling resources they offer.

Or perhaps you have already walked that journey with Jesus and want to help other women navigate toward healing. If you have a passion to work with those who have experienced trauma, let your church know. Are you a licensed counselor? If so, reach out to your local PRC to see whether there are needs you could meet with your training and skill set.

Prayer

Father, heal the brokenness in my own heart. Transform the trauma in my life, and help me feel Your love for me in the places that hurt the most. Open opportunities for me to bring healing and hope to others who have faced trauma. Give me wisdom to be a vessel of Your grace in their lives and an expression of Your love to those around me. Help those who have experienced the trauma of rape to find healing. Give those who are pregnant the strength to choose life and find restoration in You. Strengthen Your church to bear witness to Your transformative love, grace, forgiveness, and healing. Be with us and in us today and every day. Amen.

Section 3

Holistic Health

How Pregnancy Centers Support
Mental and Sexual Health

Hannah's Story

Hannah's homeschool graduation wasn't going to be the big event that most high school seniors experience, but she was excited nonetheless. Raised in a strict Christian home, she was ready for freedom from her parents' rules, especially since she'd always felt like the black sheep of the family. She'd never been afraid to push the limits of what they believed to be acceptable behavior, and throughout high school she found ways to increasingly exercise her independence.

Hannah's outlook and actions caused a lot of tension in her family as her behavior began to spiral out of control. Because Hannah wasn't the only child at home, her parents feared her choices would negatively influence her siblings. When her parents expressed their concern, their conversations turned into heated arguments. Since Hannah was old enough to be on her own, her parents finally asked her to leave.

Faced with the possibility of being homeless, she turned to Derek, her boyfriend of a few months, for a place to stay. He was hardly the kind of man she wanted to marry, but moving in with him was a chance to enjoy being wild and free for once in her life.

Hannah's parents warned her about teen pregnancy and cautioned her about her lifestyle, but she would tell them, "That'll never happen to me."

Hannah wasn't ignorant about teen pregnancy, and she felt confident she wouldn't become a statistic. Sure, she was rebellious, but she was still from a Christian homeschool background, and it just didn't seem real that she could ever be one of "those girls."

But before long, Hannah couldn't say "those girls" anymore. Telling herself she would never get pregnant with Derek's baby wasn't enough. Here she was, another teenager alone in a bathroom, staring at two lines.

Her wild and carefree feeling was replaced by the fear she felt about her pregnancy and Derek's abusive and immature behavior. It was clear he had no intention of changing or providing for a family.

"Just take care of it," he told her flippantly, hardly looking up from his video game. "You can borrow my car; the keys are on the table." Derek returned to his screen.

Hannah wanted to scream and throw something at him, but she had to take a deep breath, be strong, and think about her own life. She grabbed the keys and left for the clinic.

Inside the abortion clinic, Hannah robotically filled out the paperwork. She felt like this just *had* to be done.

Various people from her past flashed in front of her. Surely her youth pastor would be in shock, the homeschool group would be ashamed, and her family already made her feel like an outcast. She didn't have many people left to turn to. She could handle this abortion on her own better than she could stand the judgment and shame from her family and friends.

"We have to perform an ultrasound to determine the gestation of the fetus before we can prescribe the appropriate abortion procedure. Would you like to see the ultrasound?" asked the nurse.

Hannah nodded apprehensively.

But when the time came, they didn't turn the screen in her direction. She never saw the ultrasound of her baby. They said she measured seven weeks, so a chemical abortion was still possible.

Soon this will all be over, she thought.

Hannah swallowed the first pill, waited the prescribed amount of time, then swallowed the second one.

Hannah's pregnancy ended, and it wasn't long before her shallow relationship with Derek ended too. There was no way it could sustain the emotional weight of her abortion. Hannah couch-surfed for a few months before returning to her parents' house. During that time, her mental health began to deteriorate. She slumped into a deep depression and began drowning her pain with alcohol. She did her best to hide her struggles and her growing addiction from her family, but she couldn't maintain secrecy for long.

It took eight months for Hannah to open up to her family about the painful experience of her chemical abortion. It took a lot of courage, but the alternative was continuing to carry her burden alone. She knew she needed help—someone to help her carry the weight of the past and overcome her new addiction.

Hannah's family was heartbroken by her confession, but they also wanted her to heal. They assured her they would be there for her however they could, but their actual help was slow in coming. Hannah sensed their words and encouragement were empty. Unsupported, she fell deeper into despair.

Any time she saw a toddler, she found herself thinking of her baby and wondering what her life could have been like if she had made a different choice. Her depression intensified, and she soon lost all motivation to better her life. She felt like she was worthless and deserved all the pain, suffering, and mental torment. She was stuck in a cycle of emotional poverty.

Somehow she remembered that, years before, she'd heard of a pregnancy center in her town that offered after-abortion care. She knew she had to reach out for help in some way. She found out that the PRC offered a Bible study and began attending to try to understand why she felt so helpless. Hannah was familiar with the Bible, but for some reason nothing seemed to connect with her deepest feelings of pain. She finished the study, but she still didn't find healing.

Numb, isolated, and anxious, Hannah was desperate to feel anything at all. She wanted to fill the void in her heart, but she didn't know where to turn and longed for connection. Her longtime friend, Steven, was a comfort to her and was always there when she needed him. One night, in her vulnerability and need to be held, Hannah and Steven had sex.

This resulted in her second unplanned pregnancy. But this time Hannah knew she needed the support of good community. She decided to seek help at the same pregnancy center where she'd attended the abortion-recovery classes and Bible study.

"I can't go through the isolation again," she told the client advocate in their counseling session.

Determined to avoid the pain of her last decision, Hannah decided she could raise a child with the help of her new friends at the pregnancy center and the support of her family. Hannah's client advocate walked with her through the months leading up to the birth of her daughter. Together they unpacked the pain and scars left from her abortion, as well as the feelings of rejection, judgment, and shame she had experienced from her family, friends, and previous faith community.

To her relief, Hannah discovered that those she had expected to be judgmental toward her ended up being some of her biggest supporters. The pregnancy center staff helped her connect with a church that welcomed her with open arms. There she joined a chapter of Embrace Grace (see chapter 11), a national organization that helps single moms experience the lavish love of God. Hannah's depression lifted as she became more connected in her new networks, and she overcame her excessive use of alcohol. She no longer needed to numb her pain, because Christ had removed it. Her mind and heart finally found healing.

The church further surprised her by throwing her a huge baby shower, giving her supplies she needed for her new baby. Plus, they constantly reinforced the reality that Hannah was absolutely loved, valued, cherished, and accepted by her heavenly Father. She had always thought that God would kick her out and be done with her, but through the pregnancy center and the local church, she found the dazzling good news that God welcomes, heals, and embraces anyone who comes to Him.

———————————

This final section discusses unique challenges to women who find themselves sexually active, taking the abortion pill, or feeling the regret of an abortion. Women's health should include an understanding of healthy sexuality, resources for when someone changes her mind about chemical abortion, and the knowledge that there is always hope to heal after an abortion.

Chapter 7

Healthy Sexuality

Creating Supportive and Healthy Relationships

*"Christianity provides a deeper meaning to sex that
the world seeks but cannot find on its own."*

With each step that brought her closer to the abortion clinic, Katie felt her anxiety rise. *Am I pregnant? Who is the father? Can I keep this baby? How will my life change? Can I still be a dancer if I have a kid? Will I be able to go to college next fall?*

The weight of a million other unanswered questions added to the sensation of boulders being stacked on her shoulders each time her foot hit the pavement. She could hardly look up, and with an audible sigh, she mumbled, "My life is over."

"Are you okay?" A voice broke Katie's despairing train of thought. "You seem pretty down. I'm Sandra with Sidewalk Advocates for Life."

Katie was caught off guard by the kindness in Sandra's eyes and encouraged by the thought that maybe someone would help answer the countless questions swirling in her brain.

"If you'd like a free pregnancy test and ultrasound, the local pregnancy center has a medical van parked just over there. They can answer any questions you may have and give you information about resources that are available to you," Sandra said.

She gestured toward a brightly colored van with the words "Free & Confidential" on the back. When Katie peeked inside, the bus looked like a mobile doctor's office, but it felt significantly more comfortable and welcoming. There was comfy seating, an exam bed, and flat-screen TVs hooked up to an ultrasound machine. Their medical license was displayed on the wall behind Steph, a nurse, where she sat across from Jan, a social worker.

"Let's start with confirming your pregnancy," Steph suggested.

Katie went to a restroom located in the back of the bus to take the medical-grade pregnancy test.

"As we wait for the results, we would love to hear your story, if you feel comfortable sharing it with us," Jan said.

After taking a deep breath to calm her nerves, Katie began.

"My mom passed away a few months ago, and that rocked my world. I don't have any other family in the area, so I've been renting a place with a friend of mine." Katie's eyes searched the floor, and she swallowed hard before continuing. "Over the last few months, I've slept with a few different guys. It's nice to have someone close for a little while, but honestly, it's been really hard for me too. I'm not in a committed relationship. In fact, none of the guys I was with ever even called me again after they left. They just came over for one night, and I haven't seen them since. I didn't even want to have sex with them, but I felt like I didn't really have a choice."

Katie broke into soft sobs as she fought to regain her composure.

"I don't know who the father would even be," she said as a tear slid down her face. "I'm a high school senior, and I really want to become a professional dancer. I'm afraid that if I'm pregnant, I won't be able to do anything because I won't qualify for any scholarships. I don't have family around or a good job, and I don't know how I could go to college if I had a kid."

A quiet beep from a timer let the nurse know that the pregnancy test was complete. Steph glanced from the result to Katie, who was pulling another tissue from the box.

"The test is negative," Steph said.

Katie's stunned, tear-stained eyes met Steph's.

"Really?" she said.

Katie's relief was palpable. She wasn't pregnant after all, and the weight of facing the choices of an unplanned pregnancy lifted.

"I want you to know that you are loved for who you are," Jan told Katie. "You are valuable as you are. This is true because you are made in the image of God and you have intrinsic value as a human being. Your value doesn't increase or decrease based on your actions or relationships."

Jan went on to share other encouraging words before circling back to address something Katie had shared earlier.

> ## Your value doesn't increase or decrease based on your actions or relationships.

"You mentioned that you felt like you had to sleep with those guys—as if you 'didn't have a choice.' I hope you know that you never have to sleep with a guy if you don't want to; you always have the right to say no. You can set relational boundaries to help protect yourself from being used by others. You are worth someone's full love and commitment, and a true gentleman will recognize that and value you enough to stick with you through all the craziness that life might throw at you. He won't force or manipulate you into having sex. He will wait for you to be ready."

"This is crazy!" Katie exclaimed. "Why have I never heard this before?"

"Heard what?" Steph asked.

"That I could say no! I literally have never been told that I could tell a guy no when it came to sex. I've always thought I just had to."

"You always have the choice to say yes or no to anything," Steph said. "No matter what circumstance you face in life, there are always options; that's what makes it a choice. But the hard thing about choices is that you cannot choose the consequences of those choices. Sometimes the consequences carry a far heavier weight than we could ever imagine."

Katie was in shock. She had no idea people could care for a stranger so much. Now her mind started to swirl with a million new questions regarding faith, hope, love, and what it means to make relational boundaries.

"Can we pray for you before you leave?" Jan asked.

Together the three women prayed for Katie's life, specifically for wisdom and direction in her future educational and relational decisions.

"Thank you so much!" Katie said as she hugged the two ladies. She walked away from the bus, head held high for the first time in quite a while, knowing that she was empowered to choose. She could choose to say no or yes, and she had people to call if she needed to talk. Now her future was fully in her hands. Her face found the warmth of the sunshine, she inhaled deeply, and she smiled.

Voices from Culture

It might come as a surprise that Katie had never heard she could set boundaries. But the numbers reveal she is not alone.

A key study from the CDC, the National Survey of Family Growth, confirms that between 2011 and 2015, 16.3 percent of females and 18.5 percent of males did not receive formal instruction through sex education on how to say no to sex.[1]

Additionally, our culture is sending some very mixed messages to young men and women. In Netflix shows like *Sex Education*, *Riverdale*, and *New Girl*, everyone is either having sex or trying to have sex. And if they're not having sex, they're talking about it.

There's the ability to access porn with a click from any device. From advertising to music videos to song lyrics, sex has saturated our culture across every digital medium. Its influence is inescapable.

The purpose of this chapter is not to debate the best sex education course or some of the more nuanced sex-related issues that the church is facing (e.g., porn, LGBTQ issues). Other experts can speak in more depth on these topics. Our focus is geared toward the idea that Christianity provides a deeper meaning to sex that the world is desperately seeking but not finding. We want to help you make that connection for your youth and single adults, as well as focus on how your church can engage young people and singles on the topic of sex and risk avoidance—on issues ranging from STIs to abortion.

A Look at the Numbers

There are more singles in our country than ever before. In 2017, the US Census Bureau reported there were 110.6 million unmarried people over the age of eighteen—that's 45.2 percent of the American adult population.[2]

Additionally, the Census Bureau looked at the average age for marriage from 1890 to 2020. It found that in the 1950s, the average age for marriage was twenty-three for men and twenty for women. By 2020, it had climbed to thirty for men and twenty-eight for women.[3]

With the majority of people getting married closer to their thirties and the increasing cultural pressure to engage in sex much earlier, there's a lot to wrestle with when it comes to sex for singles and young adults.

Author Lauren Winner, in her book *Real Sex*, notes that "as the church, we need to ask whether the starting point for a scriptural witness on sex is the isolated quotation of 'thou shalt not,' or whether a scriptural ethic of sex begins instead with the totality of the Bible, the narrative of God's redeeming love and humanity's attempt to reflect that through our institutions and practices."[4]

When we talk about sex within this larger framework, we can see the masterful work of a God who uses human sexuality to paint a glorious picture for His creation. Sexuality is part of who we are as humans yet too often is left unexplained.

In fact, as early as the 1990s, in a study from Albion College and Illinois State University, professors surveyed two hundred college-aged virgins. The most-stated reason for holding on to their virginity was "I haven't been in love or been in a primary relationship long enough." Religious and moral motivations for remaining abstinent were much lower on the list.[5] This implies that a Christian ethic hasn't been compelling when it comes to sexual relations.

The Biblical Story of Sex

In his book *After Virtue*, Alasdair MacIntyre states, "[We] can only answer the question 'What am I to do?' if [we] can answer the prior question 'Of what story or stories do I find myself a part?'"[6]

How can we understand what it means to be human? Or how can we engage our bodies and sexuality in a way that fulfills the purpose and design for which they were made? The pursuit of an answer requires us to understand not only the story of healthy relationships outlined in Scripture but also the part we play as characters within that story.

The truth is, the biblical view of sex is far more intentional and beautiful than even the most glamorous narratives the world offers. The problem is, sex has become distorted by sin, and in turn, the way the church often approaches the topic makes it feel taboo, dirty, or shameful. Often the church's position is "Don't do it until you're married." End of story. But the narrative of our life experience is significantly more complex.

Ken Robertson is the pastor of the International Anglican Church in Colorado Springs, Colorado. He offers a contrast between the cultural and Christian stories of sex.

"The cultural story basically says that sex is about us: it is something we take, for our own pleasure. This leads to people using and being used and ultimately makes sex selfish. It cheapens our dignity when we take sex and discard the person, or when we are discarded."

The truth is, sex is not just about the body; it's more intricate. And the story about sex doesn't start with Paul in the New Testament; it begins with the giving of a gift. It begins in Genesis 1 and 2, during the very formation of life itself when God designed humanity, bodies, and marriage.

"In the first chapters of Genesis, we learn that God created a relationship between Adam and Eve. This relationship is the context in which sex is first understood," Winner writes in *Real Sex*. "In a graphic speech, Adam speaks of his and Eve's becoming one flesh.... It captures an all-encompassing, overarching oneness—when they marry, husband and wife enter an institution that points them toward familial, domestic, emotional, and spiritual unity."[7]

> The biblical view of sex is far more intentional and beautiful than even the most glamorous narratives the world offers.

God set up the idea from the very beginning that sex is reserved for the context of marriage and reinforced this truth throughout Scripture—from Song of Songs, which paints a picture of sexuality restored by grace, to the Mosaic law, which was written to help order and reinforce the sexual practices put forth in Genesis. And in 1 and 2 Corinthians, Paul addressed sexual ethics from sexual immorality to marriage. In 1 Corinthians 6:16 he wrote, "The two will become one flesh," a reference back to Genesis, reminding us of God's consistent plan for sex throughout history.

Within the marriage relationship, God designed an image of the relationship humans are to have with Him. "[Marriage] is a 'living picture' of the kind of relationship we were made to have with Him: both intimate and committed," Pastor Robertson explains. "That's why sex is only meant for marriage: it is intimacy in the midst of commitment. God draws us close and doesn't let go, affirming our dignity. Sex in the midst of marriage does the same: it is the ultimate intimacy, in the midst of the ultimate commitment. That marriage commitment, as Ephesians 5 says, is like a big sign pointing us back to that relationship with God."

If you disconnect intimacy from commitment, you fall into a selfishness that leads you right back into the cultural story. God does not use us and will not be used by us—He values us, and Himself, too much for that.

Talking about Healthy Sexuality

So how do we start getting this message across—most importantly to younger generations?

While most middle school and high school students have gone through a sex-ed class, it was at most a few hours a day for a week or less. If their parents, church leaders, youth pastors, or other trusted authority figures didn't talk to them about sex, then the rest of their education came from the larger culture we just mentioned. Young people are learning from plenty of other venues: Netflix, Pornhub, Snapchat—just to name a few. These mediums are all educating teens and young adults about sex. And they're listening.

The National Survey of Family Growth surveyed teens about their sexual activity and sex education. From 2011 to 2015, the average age American males and females lost their virginity was seventeen.[8] Less than 15 percent of males and females ages twenty to twenty-four are virgins, and it drops below 5 percent for males and females twenty-five to twenty-nine.[9]

The National Campaign to Prevent Teen and Unplanned Pregnancy estimates that 80 percent of unmarried adults ages eighteen to twenty-nine who identify as evangelicals have had sex. And 64 percent have done so within the last year.[10]

Additionally, Katie's story from the beginning of the chapter highlights the fact that many teens are not educated on healthy sexuality and relational boundaries, which can have sweeping consequences not only in the emotional realm but also in the physical arena.

The CDC recently released their 2019 *Sexually Transmitted Disease Surveillance Report*:

- Combined cases of syphilis, gonorrhea, and chlamydia reached an all-time high in the United States in 2019.
- Chlamydia increased 3 percent, setting a new record, with more than 1.8 million cases (the most ever reported to the CDC). It is now the most common sexually transmitted infection (STI) in the nation.
- Almost two-thirds of the cases were among fifteen- to twenty-four-year-olds.[11]

Healthy Conversations

Jason Orona works with teens in high schools all across southern Colorado. He is the director of a sex education program that works directly with a local pregnancy resource center. The program is a weeklong course in which he and his staff educate students on healthy relationships.

"I had a student once tell me that abstinence was not doing drugs or alcohol," he said.

This comment motivates him to do what he does. He works with his students to promote the idea that healthy relationships are the first step to preventing many of the unwanted consequences of sex: STIs, abuse, unplanned pregnancy, and abortion.

"Our job is prevention," he said. "Our job is to put the pregnancy center out of business. If we set people up well, the need for a PRC will become obsolete. The more we educate students on healthy relationships and healthy sex, [the more] we remove the need for pregnancy centers and Planned Parenthood."

Learning about healthy sexuality diminishes the need for abortion because if people are in healthy relationships and women feel supported, even if they are facing an unplanned pregnancy, they are less likely to choose abortion.

Orona recommends that parents and teens have ongoing conversations about sex and what healthy relationships are built on—including boundaries. These interactions have to be grace filled and full of forgiveness and understanding.

Orona says that telling someone not to do something isn't the best way to approach the topic. Instead, we need to tell the story that sex was created for good. Intimacy isn't a bad thing; in fact, God created it as a plan for procreation and our enjoyment (Gen. 2:21–25).

But this is not a one-time conversation.

"You have to start building rapport and trust. Creating an everyday language on the subject so it's not taboo," he said. "You could start by talking about Netflix shows, asking what [your children] think about how the teens handle sex on these shows. It's all about creating a safe space to start talking about it."

If you aren't sure where to begin, consider asking your local PRC about the extent of their community outreach and education efforts. Here are some questions to consider:

- What and where do they teach in your community?
- If the PRC is not the one teaching in your schools, what is being taught to young people about sex?
- Is the sex education in your schools offering students a full understanding and biblical expression of God's purpose for sex in the context of marriage?
- If not, does your church provide an alternative that teaches students to value their bodies?
- Is your church equipping parents to engage their children in healthy and ongoing conversations about sexuality?

Wondering Where to Start?

As you contemplate this topic and the role of your church, be sensitive to the different perspectives and approaches that PRCs, the church, parents, teens, and singles will each bring to this subject. Remember that there is forgiveness, redemption, and the opportunity to change at any moment because we always have healing and hope through Christ. The more we engage in healthy dialogue about this topic, the more we can engage the culture, set women and men up for success in their relationships and parenting, and promote their ability to see their own invaluable self-worth.

To normalize conversations in the home and provide biblical guidance, it's important for churches to lead the way by talking about sex in healthy ways from the pulpit and within youth and young adult groups.

Orona noted that the church can begin the conversation with good theological information about sex. Here are some ways pastors and churches can start this process.

Remove Stigma and Shame

If you're a pastor, pray for wisdom as you approach your leadership, your congregation, and individuals. Gently request that any judgment or condemnation in conversations about sex be replaced with grace, forgiveness, and compassion.

Get Leadership Involved in the Conversation

The head pastor can talk to the staff about the topic and answer questions so everyone is equipped to address it. Explaining the "why" behind the initiative—saving a generation of young people from future hurt—will inspire people to work through any discomfort.

Evaluate with Your Staff

- How have we seen sex stigmatized in our church? How can we change this?
- What words are we using to talk about sex that aren't helpful?
- What resources can we recommend to parents, young adults, and teens?
- What messages do teens, singles, engaged couples, or unmarried pregnant woman in our church receive about sex?

- How can we better talk about God's design for relationships, marriage, and sex?
- How can we support sexual risk avoidance?

Pay Attention to Terminology

Words like *purity*, *promiscuity*, and *virginity* all have emotional and oftentimes harmful connotations. They can imply that once failure happens, there is a lasting stain that cannot be removed even by God's grace. We have to find ways to discuss identity and value that are not connected to one's sexual status, that remove the shame associated with these words, and that use language that conveys worth in God's eyes.

Be Accessible and Organic

The topic of sex can't just be a sermon series or limited to one topic like pornography or LGBTQ issues. It also can't just be "in relation to marriage" or geared toward couples. Don't isolate single people from this relevant conversation.

The reason we need to discuss human sexuality often and broadly is to inform the "why." Pastor Robertson explained: "Why would God put these rules around sex? Because we miss God's invitation to learn more about Him, and we damage ourselves and others when we do it any other way. Sex is His gift, but it's a powerful one. He is kind enough to give us directions on how to use it properly."

Have Inclusive Conversations

The more you can include everyone in your congregation in the conversation, the better the dialogue. While men or women might feel safer discussing certain topics with the same gender, it is important not to create division or separate narratives on the topic of sex within the church. Single people may find the subject more relevant than they would like to admit, and older generations can provide valuable perspectives. You can't exile singles who might be having sex, people in second marriages, or individuals going through a divorce.

Be mindful of how your church addresses both genders. For too long, "modesty culture" has made women feel as if they are doing something wrong or that they have to take responsibility for how men view them. The church needs to hold men accountable for their attitudes and actions. If we're talking about sex, men are involved as well. This doesn't mean conversations always have to be held with men and women together, but both are integral to the dialogue.

Engage Singles

Many Christians have elevated marriage as the climactic moment in our faith. We've put marriage on a pedestal, and we honor it above singleness. But if we talk about marriage and singleness in a healthy way, then we're also talking about sex in a healthy way. Singles should not be marginalized within the church, nor should they be forgotten when conversations about sex arise. Singles must navigate a very complex and difficult journey in a culture that constantly invites and pressures them to partake in its view of sexuality.

Engage Teens

Youth pastors don't have to be experts on all topics relating to sex; they can invite someone from their local PRC to talk about healthy relationships, boundaries, emotional and spiritual relationships, and risk avoidance. Sexuality is the biggest topic teens are navigating. It's real, and it's not something we can skip over or be embarrassed about. Normalizing these difficult topics helps teens talk with trusted adults maturely and honestly.

Get Talking

While every church is unique and may approach the information and discussion differently, here are some options to get the conversation started:

- Host a conference with experts (live or virtual), or hold town hall meetings.
- Invite someone from your local PRC or another speaker to talk about issues related to sex, relationships, and marriage.
- Host a book club or small group discussions.
- Equip small group leaders with information to take back to their groups, including a church-wide campaign.
- Share your church's view of biblical sexuality, and walk through the reasons you hold these views.

Reflecting the Father's Heart

Paul warned against the "cunning and craftiness" of culture and the false narratives that try to destroy the body of Christ; he continued by admonishing the church to be "speaking the truth in love" so believers could grow toward maturity and become a truer reflection of Jesus (Eph. 4:14–15).

In Colossians 4:6, Paul also admonished the church to "let your conversation be always full of grace, seasoned with salt, so that you may know how to answer everyone."

Too often, well-intended Christians either focus on the truth of God's Word—seemingly without love or compassion—or emphasize only love without sharing the whole truth of Scripture. But God calls us to share both: His truth combined with love brings maturity and the holistic life God designed for humanity.

Conversations about sexuality, sexual risk avoidance, and healthy relationships may not be easy to engage in at first. We must enter these conversations prayerfully, seasoned with grace, truth, and love, without triggering feelings of shame, judgment, or fear. The gospel is wisdom. The church can point people to the truest story ever—God sent Jesus to redeem us and offer us the deepest fulfillment.

Ask the Lord to open doors of opportunity for you to engage the young people in your home and church with meaningful, honest, safe, true, and loving conversations about God's design for sex.

Prayer

Heavenly Father, author of life and creator of all good things, help me better understand Your design for relationships and sex. Help me communicate Your truth with Your heart of deep, compassionate love. Give me eyes to see the young people in my community as You see them, and help me and my church to interact with them in ways that will be meaningful to them. Shape my heart to love them as You love them and to speak to those around me words of life that come from You. Amen.

Chapter 8

Supportive Fathers

Mentoring Men to Become Invested Fathers

"It takes two to tango."

Pearl Bailey, singer

Leo's keys swayed from the ignition in his car. His mind swayed too, back and forth, as he started this morning's drive. He tightened his grip on the wheel with his left hand and reached for the keys with his right. Oddly enough, calming those swinging keys and guiding the wheel gave him the sense, even if just for a moment, that he could actually control something in his life.

His girlfriend, Laura, sat motionless in the passenger seat. Her silence was suffocating. Staring out the window, she tried her best to remember the good times from her and Leo's relationship, but she couldn't escape her reflection in the glass and the reality that had led them to where they were now. Her eyes traced the endless line on the side of the highway. It was a constant reminder of those two lines on the pregnancy test she wished she could erase. Laura had recently gotten the job she'd always wanted, and a baby was the very last thing in her plans.

"I just can't have a baby right now," she repeated emphatically whenever it came up.

Leo felt the fear too, but he had always wanted to be a father and could envision starting a family with Laura, the woman he loved. Leo had passion and opinions and even dared at times to admit to himself that he already loved this child.

Still, when he spoke with Laura about the baby, all that came out of his mouth was "I'm with you, and I want whatever you think is best for you."

What else could he say? It was her body, her choice. What did it matter now?

Leo parked the car in front of the clinic. He wanted to show Laura affection, but he still questioned himself at every turn, doubting his role and his place in such a painful process.

"I'm sorry, but we can't perform your abortion here," the abortion clinic employee informed them. "Your pregnancy has progressed past the time when we can legally perform abortions, so you'll have to go out of state."

After twenty-two weeks' gestation, abortion is illegal in most states, but Laura found the phone number to an abortion clinic in New Mexico that legally provided abortions up to birth. Laura walked out to the parking lot, mustering up the courage to make the call. Leo stood nearby in silence as she made another appointment for the following Friday.

Laura and Leo both knew they would need to use up vacation days from work to get this procedure done. Not in a million years would they have imagined using their hard-earned vacation days for the purpose of an abortion. But they had no other choice. A baby right now just wasn't right for them.

A longer drive, more silence, more swaying keys, more looking out the window, trying to escape their reality. The drive to the new clinic was even heavier than the last, and walking through the door felt even harder than the first time. Leo sat next to Laura in the lobby as she filled out the paperwork. He tried to stay calm, but when the nurse called Laura back into the operating room, he was overwhelmed by the atmosphere and all the sad eyes around him, staring down at the floor.

He sat for a moment, searching aimlessly on his phone for something to distract his mind, but all he could hear was his heart beating louder and louder in his ears. The sound of his own heartbeat became too much to bear. It reminded him of the heartbeat of his baby that would soon be gone. He stood up and darted outside for some fresh air. As he paced in the parking lot of the abortion clinic, an unfamiliar voice caught his attention and brought his mind back down to earth.

"Excuse me," said a woman with a warm smile. "I'd like to give you something, for you and your partner."

She held out a white gift bag and waited with a calming presence. Leo reached out for the gift. Anything to take his mind off what was happening inside the clinic. He opened the bag and glanced inside, seeing a few little items and a pamphlet; the word *hope* jumped off the page as though it were alive. It was such a simple word, but it hit him with great force in that moment. He wanted hope, but he needed to guard his heart. He closed the bag quickly and simply said, "Thank you."

Just as Leo was about to walk away with his gift bag, the woman held out her hand and introduced herself.

"I'm Marta," she said.

Leo shook her hand, and for the first time in a long time, he felt like talking about what had been happening inside his heart. "Why are you doing this, Marta? Why stand out here and hand out gifts to people? I mean, you know what we're here for."

"I'm here because I want everyone who walks through those doors to know they're not alone," she told him. "I've found they often feel hopeless, and if no one else will give them hope, then I will. There *is* hope, and there *are* alternatives, and I'm here because I want you to know that. We're parked right over there, and we have a lot of resources to help."

She pointed to a bright-green van advertising free ultrasounds and pregnancy tests. "The local pregnancy center owns that vehicle, and licensed nurses and social workers are there to help any woman who wants to know about *all* her options before making a final decision about her pregnancy."

"Why do they do that?" Leo asked. "I mean, I've seen those self-righteous picketers who want to damn me and Laura to hell for doing what's best for us right now. They like to hang around these places, yelling at people. I saw some of them at the last clinic we were at, but y'all don't seem like them at all."

"No, shouting and protesting tend to erect walls rather than allow us to show you we're here to help you," Marta said in a kind tone. "We genuinely care about you because we understand that there are really painful and complicated reasons why you're making this decision."

The sound of a slamming door broke the calm between Marta and Leo. Startled, they both turned quickly toward the clinic. Laura stood there, a medical band around her wrist and a bandage on her arm where they had drawn blood to confirm her pregnancy. Her face showed a mixture of anxiety, fear, and confusion.

Leo sprinted over to her in panic, stopping just short of an embrace. "What's going on?" he asked.

Tears filled Laura's eyes, and her hands were shaking. "I asked to see my ultrasound, but they wouldn't let me see it. I thought I could feel the baby move. Then they took me back into the operating room to wait for the doctor, but I just couldn't. I couldn't stay there alone. I need you."

She tried to catch her breath and maintain her composure, but her tears gave way to sobbing. Laura buried her face in Leo's chest as the emotions she had been afraid to acknowledge for so long began to break free. Sadness, fear, anger, and so much more erupted all at once. It was like the feelings that once held her captive started to set her free.

"Babe, I'm with you," he whispered into her ear. "It's gonna be okay."

Leo's words calmed Laura down. Once she caught her breath, he looked into her eyes and added, "Those folks over there—they have a

van where we could get a free ultrasound. We could see our baby—
right now. This lady, Marta, said there's a bunch of ways they can help
us. Also, they don't seem angry with us for being here. We can always
go back and get the abortion after we meet with them. I think we
should check it out. What do you say?"

"Okay," she whispered, knowing in her heart that she needed to
see her baby before settling on her decision.

> Shouting and protesting tend to erect
> walls rather than allow us to show
> you we're here to help you.

Marta walked the couple over to the mobile medical unit and
introduced them to the sonographer and social worker on board.
Neither Laura nor Leo had ever seen a mobile doctor's office, but that's
exactly what the van was like, except that it was much more comfortable and welcoming than a typical medical building.

Stepping on board, they noticed the soft touch of the medical-
grade vinyl seats that formed a small counseling area near the door.
Next to the seats on the right of the bus was an exam table, slightly
reclined, facing the flat-screen TV at the front of the bus. On the left
side of the bus was a counter with an ultrasound machine, which
projected the ultrasound image onto the TV for the client and her
guests to see. At the rear of the bus, clients could use the restroom and
produce a sample for the pregnancy test. Everything necessary for a
clinical-grade pregnancy test and ultrasound was neatly packed into
this twenty-five-foot Mercedes Sprinter.

"Let's take a look and see how far along you are," the sonographer
said as she gently covered Laura's pregnant stomach with cool blue gel.
Unlike in the abortion clinic, the ultrasound screen was right in front

of Laura so she could see everything if she wanted to. Gray and white lines appeared as the wand slid slowly across her belly.

"Whoa!" Laura exclaimed as she saw an arm waving at her. Her baby measured twenty-three weeks. The baby's development shown on-screen was far beyond anything she'd imagined. Until that moment, she had thought of her pregnancy only as a problem, not as a person with little fingers and toes.

Laura's unexpected reaction brought Leo to the edge of his seat as he excitedly leaned closer to the TV. A smile, larger than Laura had ever seen, transformed his entire face, and tears tinged with joy ran from his eyes as he touched the outline of his baby on the screen.

"That's my little boy ... my baby." He took a deep breath before turning to her. "We made that!"

The baby jumped and even appeared to do a little somersault.

"Look, Laura! He's even hyper like me!" Leo grinned.

For weeks they had only been dealing with stress. Now they found themselves caught up in bursts of laughter and true joy—something that neither of them had allowed to spill out in far too long. It sounded like a beloved yet somehow-forgotten melody breaking through the agony of silence they had been trapped in.

Laura turned her attention from the ultrasound screen to Leo's face and apprehensively said, "I never knew you wanted the baby. You never really said anything about it."

Leo felt a dagger through his heart. He felt shame, even though he had wanted to say something all along.

"I didn't think I had the right to say anything," he said, looking into Laura's eyes. His smile fell as he continued, "It just wrecked me inside. I wanted our baby, but I wanted to respect you and your choice. What right does a guy like me have, I mean, to tell a girl I love what to do with her body? At least that's what everyone told me. That's why

I stayed out of it. I figured you needed to decide what would be best for you. But I love you, and I want to be with you, and I want to be a dad to our baby. I'll do whatever it takes to have you both in my life. I don't know what it takes to be a good father, but I want to try. I'll do the best I can."

Laura was in shock. Before Leo said those words, she had no idea that he was willing to stay with her if she chose life. Somehow she'd always thought that it was either Leo or the baby, and she couldn't imagine life without him. Was it really possible to have him *and* her child?

"You know," the nurse said, "pregnancy centers offer parenting classes where you can learn how to get on your feet and develop your understanding of what it means to be a parent."

She gave Laura and Leo the numbers to some organizations near their hometown that had men's mentoring and fatherhood support groups, along with continued care for mothers and families.

Gazing at his child's mother, Leo admired the lines of her strong and beautiful face. His attention turned to the medical band around Laura's wrist, and he remembered that the abortion clinic was right outside.

"Do you have scissors?" he asked the nurse.

Laura understood exactly what he was thinking. "I got it," she said as she ripped the abortion clinic's medical bracelet off.

"Who needs scissors when you have willpower?" she said with a confident smile.

As they stepped out of the van together, the pregnancy center staff handed them a card, along with a list of local organizations that would pick up where they had left off. They gave them something else too: those beautiful ultrasound photos of their baby boy.

"If you need anything else—anything—please give us a call. We are here to support you, even from afar."

Leo gave Marta an extra-long hug as he wiped away his tears of joy and gratitude. Laura couldn't stop looking at the ultrasound photos, and she also couldn't stop looking over at Leo.

"I never knew you wanted this baby," she told him. "I wish I'd known sooner."

He glanced over and replied, "I'm sorry. I didn't want to get in the way, but I can see now how my silence made you think I wanted an abortion. I'll learn how to be there for you and our baby. I want to be a better man, for both of you. I know I failed you by not speaking up, by putting it all on you. I won't do that again."

He opened the car door for her, and she sat down with her gift bag and photos in her lap. As Leo drove off, he let those keys sway and didn't clench the wheel so tightly. Instead of looking out the window, Laura gazed over at Leo, thinking of how they would use those vacation days in the future, as a family, to show their little boy the ocean for the very first time.

A Father's Voice

Tragically, culture told Leo that he had no voice in the matter, and he believed it. But Leo was born to love and protect. By going against his own nature, he caused a destructive, almost deadly rift between himself and the family he desired. But Leo found his voice and was ready to do whatever it took to support and protect the ones he loved. Because of the help of people like Marta, he no longer had to be unsure about the role he could play as a father and partner.

Thousands of men find themselves in Leo's shoes every day. It's often easy to forget, but for every woman facing an unplanned pregnancy, there is also a man. As we saw in a previous chapter, some men do pressure women into abortion, but there are others who feel like they don't have the right to stand for life. The topic of abortion frames the conversation around the woman and the baby, but both pro-choice and pro-life narratives often exclude the father. Consequently, many men feel as if they shouldn't have a say in decisions related to the life of their unborn child. Much of society tells them to stay out of it—and they listen.

In an episode of HBO's *Girls*, the character Mimi-Rose says in passing to her boyfriend, Adam, that she can't go for a run with him because she had an abortion the day before.

She says it so casually it takes him a minute to process it.

"Was it mine?" he asks, shocked.

"Of course it was yours," she says. "I didn't want to talk about it beforehand; I just wanted to do it. It was a ball of cells." She shrugs.

"Isn't this a decision that people typically make together?" he asks.[1]

The exchange in this episode embodies the cultural slogan "My body, my choice." Men are told every day to stay out of the debate and the decision-making.

A survey of 210 male partners of women seeking abortions in a midwestern city found that many men actually do want to be part of the process, though. And not only do they want to be part of the process, but more than half (57 percent) would not have chosen to terminate the pregnancy.[2]

But legally, men have no say when it comes to abortion.

In the 1976 case *Planned Parenthood v. Danforth*, the Supreme Court ruled that laws requiring a spouse's consent for an abortion are unconstitutional. Even though both parties have an interest in the decision, if they disagree, the woman's position prevails. According to the court, since the woman actually carries the pregnancy, the balance weighs in her favor, preventing the father from vetoing her choice.[3]

Roland Warren, president of Care Net and former president of the National Fatherhood Initiative, noted that the "right to choose" rhetoric places the responsibility of the pregnancy outcome solely on the woman. But rights and responsibilities are inextricably linked. This means that when men are excluded from having a right to speak up for their child, they can also avoid the responsibility related to their partners' decision.

Yet the reality is, women listen to their partners and want them to be actively involved. Care Net's research supports this. In fact, 61 percent of women said they included the father of their child in making a decision about their unplanned pregnancy.[4]

> The question for men facing unplanned pregnancies is not whether they will be fathers but what kind of father will they be.

Warren went on to say, "When a woman comes to a pregnancy center, she's often asked if the father knows about the pregnancy. Often the following question is 'What does he think?' but really we should be asking, 'Why did you tell him?'

"The truth is, most women aren't hoping to hear 'I'll support any decision you make,'" he explained. "Somewhere inside her she's hoping he'll advocate for life; otherwise she would never tell him—she'd just do it. What if we could help men respond in the way women actually want? If he's an advocate for life, she's much less likely to have an abortion. If a woman comes to a pregnancy center, then [the father] needs to come too, and we need to inspire him, equip him, and help him be the advocate for life and support to her."

But if men don't have role models of committed, responsible fatherhood in their own homes, they'll end up taking their cue from the strong, clear messages of culture, which tell them they're not needed and the choice is up to women.

Society as a whole is paying dearly for this message.

"We need to go back to the Word of God and see how God responds to an unplanned pregnancy from a human perspective," Warren said. "When we do, we find the story of Mary's unplanned pregnancy with Jesus."

In Matthew 1:20, God called and commissioned Joseph to be a husband to Mary and a father to Jesus.* The angel speaking to Joseph first protected the sanctity of marriage and family consistent with God's design; then he affirmed the sanctity of life, saying, "Do not be afraid to take Mary home as your wife, because what is conceived in her is from the Holy Spirit."

Warren continued, "The question for men facing unplanned pregnancies is not whether they will be fathers but what kind of father will they be. Joseph is called to provide and protect, which is woven into the very nature of men. Ask any boy what he wants to be when he grows up, and he'll say he wants to do something heroic, like be a firefighter, doctor, or police officer. Men understand that the most heroic thing you can do is to protect the vulnerable. We must inspire men by informing them of the privilege and sacred honor they have of being a father."

Being pro-life from a holistic point of view means not only preserving life but also improving it. Being "pro-dad" is an often-overlooked, yet essential, part of this work. A Pew Research study found that 87 percent of males aged fifteen to forty-four with no children wanted to have them at some point.[5] Thankfully, PRCs are innovating and embracing programs that encourage and equip men as fathers.

HeartReach Pregnancy Center in Wasilla, Alaska, is just one of many pregnancy resource centers across the country that are actively mentoring men to be better fathers. Doug Prins has been the

---

*   Care Net's fatherhood program is called the Joseph Project and is modeled after the call to Joseph to provide for and protect Mary and the unplanned pregnancy they faced together.

fatherhood program manager since 2015, following years of service as a volunteer at the PRC. Their center offers four hundred different classes for men and women as they become parents and develop their parenting skills.

"Men come to us from all walks of life," Prins said. "Some are looking to just be better dads; others come out of prison and are sent to us by the courts or the Office of Children's Services. Sometimes men see our advertisement at the local DMV, or they hear about us from one of the sixty-two churches in our community that we're connected with."

Through his work, Prins found common fears men are trying to address: *Am I capable of being a father? Am I qualified? Do I have what it takes to be a dad? How would I know if I'm doing the right thing with or for my kids?*

The fear of the unknown, especially for those who've never been a dad before, is monumental. They have a new responsibility to step into, and they're not sure if they're up for the task.

"Selfishness is hard to overcome," Prins said, "but if a man can learn to become a servant to the baby's mom and to their children, families can be saved and strengthened."

This is exactly why mentoring for fathers at a PRC can be especially life changing and lifesaving.

Men come to HeartReach weekly to meet one on one with Prins and other volunteer mentors. Together they go through a variety of classes, depending on what the client needs at the time. If he's a new father facing an unplanned pregnancy, they may do the Embracing Fatherhood class or New Father by the National Fatherhood Initiative. Other resources they use include *You Have What It Takes* by John Eldredge, *Stepping Up* by Dennis Rainey, and resources by Focus on the Family, FamilyLife Today, and All Pro Dad (www.allprodad.com).

At the end of each session, the mentor asks if he can pray with and for the client.

"In eight years of mentoring men, I've only had one man say no when I asked if I could pray for him," Prins said. "Often they say yes with tears in their eyes. I always share the gospel with them, and I've seen many come to know Christ and get connected to the men's ministry at local churches."

Equipping the Church to Care for Fathers

The attitude of "I'll support whatever you decide" rather than standing up to defend truth and protect life is not unique to our culture or our place in history. We can find this first depicted in Genesis 3. Adam was with his wife when she decided to listen to the snake and cross a boundary God set. Her decision and Adam's inaction resulted, ultimately, in death and broken relationships. Sins of both commission and omission result in equal yet different consequences that weigh on the couple and have a ripple effect on the entirety of their lives.

As we've seen in this chapter, humanity has not changed much since Genesis 3. Men may still avoid the conversation but reap the consequences—whether good or bad—of their partners' decision. The choice between life and death may be determined by their action, or inaction, in the decision-making process.

Now let's imagine a young man who has just discovered his girlfriend is pregnant. Maybe he's active in his youth group. Or maybe he's never set foot in a church his entire life. Either way, he's scared and unsure where to turn for trustworthy advice. All he knows is that he loves his partner and feels the only support he has the right to give her is to say, "I'll support whatever you decide."

What would happen if we connected the same young man with an experienced and caring father—an invested Christian man who could encourage him without judgment to answer the call, like Joseph in the book of Matthew, to protect and provide for his partner, honor marriage, and parent their baby? By doing so, we give him hope and confidence that he may have never received before. Perhaps, with time, he'll become the man he's designed to be but never recognized was within him. Maybe we'll see him be a present father by changing his newborn's diapers, giving his partner a break, playing on the floor with his toddler, teaching his son to ride a bike, and working hard to provide for his family, and hopefully becoming a man of God who will lead his family well.

But how can we engage these men? What can the church do?

First, we need to initiate the conversation about life and fatherhood. So many men feel they can't be fathers because they never had fathering modeled to them, or perhaps it's all too overwhelming and they feel alone and incapable. Opening the conversation about fatherhood, unplanned pregnancy, and the value of unborn life itself can happen in youth groups, schools, and families.

Doug Prins said that some of his clients go hunting, fishing, or hiking with their mentors. If someone's story is sensitive or current, these topics may be easier to talk about while doing something together, especially something they both enjoy. Shared experiences often create the ability to engage the deeper emotional spaces within the hearts of men.

Some questions a mentor could ask a mentee include:

- Who is your role model as a father?
- What kind of father do you want to be?
- What are your goals for a family someday?
- Do you value marriage? Why or why not?

At HeartReach, men are led through SMART goals* to help them outline the path they want to walk so they have direction and some protection from abandoning their progress. This tool is used by HeartReach to help fathers think through their goals and ensure they're living up to their own goals as men and fathers as they grow.

Second, we need to change the conversation about men and fatherhood in our culture. You would think our culture would want to build up dads, show their importance, and empower them to be better men. But many conversations surrounding life issues reinforce the message that men should stay silent and distant.

"So many men have been beaten down and told they're nothing and they're unworthy or they don't matter," Prins said. "Negative voices are very hard to uproot, but we can be part of instilling positive voices into these men's lives. We tell them that God loves them, He wants to use them, and He has a purpose for their lives."

Care Net has many resources for individuals, churches, and pregnancy centers to engage men in this conversation. Some resources include *Welcoming Him*, *Dr. Dad*, and *Before She Decides*, all designed to help stimulate a holistic pro-life narrative that includes the father too.

Roland Warren said, "As a ministry model, you have to pursue men in a very different way. A woman has to go somewhere; the baby is coming no matter what, so she's either going to an abortion clinic or a pregnancy center. But the guy doesn't have to go anywhere; he could walk away. We [as the pro-life community] have to pursue him in a way that calls and missions him to be the man he was made to be."

---

*   SMART is an acronym developed by Peter Drucker meaning "specific, measurable, achievable, relevant, time-bound." You can learn more about this system by searching "SMART goals" online.

Wondering Where to Start?

Does your church have a ministry for new, teen, single, or abortion-vulnerable dads? Here are some practical steps that churches and other faith communities can take to support young men in unplanned pregnancy situations:

1. Invite husbands and fathers in your church to volunteer as mentors to younger men and fathers in your community. Ask your local PRC if their fatherhood director could train those in your church who would like to mentor men.

2. Provide opportunities for your volunteer mentors to connect with men in need, and communicate this amazing resource to your community. One-on-one mentoring is ideal, but hosting an event for men could be a way to connect men and mentors. After they're connected, the individuals can find something they both enjoy and see how the conversations open as they spend time together. Remember, it takes time to build trust and get into the deeply emotional recesses of the heart of a man in this situation. Give it time and keep pursuing him.

3. Network with local PRCs so they're aware of those who are willing to walk alongside young fathers who come through their doors.

4. Pray for your local pregnancy center. If you have a prayer group at your church, make sure someone is actively connecting with your PRC and praying for the specific needs their clients have. There is no limit to what God can do when the church is mobilized through prayer and the power of the Holy Spirit.

Chapter 11 has many more ideas about how your church can have a deeper impact on men who are vulnerable to abortion, need help recovering from a partner's abortion, or are single dads. Our country needs invested dads, and we have the power to build them up. Together we can change the statistics one father at a time.

Reflecting the Father's Heart

Scripture makes it clear that fathers are vital in a child's life, so much so that caring for the fatherless makes the short list of acts of justice that are important to God.

> Learn to do right; seek justice.
>   Defend the oppressed.
> Take up the cause of the fatherless;
>   plead the case of the widow. (Isa. 1:17)

> Defend the weak and the fatherless;
>   uphold the cause of the poor and the oppressed.
> Rescue the weak and the needy;
>   deliver them from the hand of the wicked.
>   (Ps. 82:3–4)

If God notices fatherless children and wants us to have a heart for them, then we should also have a heart for encouraging and equipping fathers. When the church rallies around men, they can become the fathers God designed them to be.

Prayer

Dear Father and Creator of all life, help those who feel silenced by our culture to find their voices to protect unborn life. Give me opportunities to support fathers and potential fathers in my community. I pray that You would surround those who face an unplanned pregnancy right now with Your compassionate love. I ask that You would bring mentors into their lives and grow them into the men You've designed them to be. Thank You for being a Father who rebuilds, restores, and resurrects life. May Your church be an avenue through which You redeem all things. Use me as part of Your plan. I ask this in Jesus' name. Amen.

Chapter 9

Abortion Pill Reversal

A Second Chance to Choose

"Ignorance is Satan's weapon, but the weapons
of God are truth and information."

Mary LeQuieu, former executive director of Care Net
of Albuquerque and chemical abortion survivor

"I'm sorry, I can't understand what you're saying. Can you repeat that?"

The receptionist closed off her ear opposite the receiver with her finger in order to focus on deciphering the frantic voice on the phone. She could hear a woman sobbing uncontrollably in the background.

"Is there anything we can do?" Luis said again to the receptionist. "We're at the abortion clinic now, and Isabella just took the first pill. As soon as we walked out of the clinic, we both regretted it. Is there anything we can do to stop this abortion?"

Just a few months before, Centro Tepeyac Women's Center became one of the more than nine hundred providers affiliated with Heartbeat International's Abortion Pill Rescue Network. Their medical staff were trained on protocol for Abortion Pill Rescue for moments like this: to help reverse the effects of the abortion pill and give mothers a second chance to choose life.

What Is the Abortion Pill?

Currently, pregnant women in the United States who want an abortion in the first ten weeks of their pregnancy are given RU-486, known as the abortion pill. This pill is different from Plan B or "the morning-after pill." Plan B is an over-the-counter drug taken immediately after unprotected sex that works by "delaying or preventing ovulation," according to the Mayo Clinic.[1] A woman taking Plan B may or may not be pregnant.

In contrast, the abortion pill protocol includes two pills to complete a chemical abortion after a confirmed pregnancy. The first pill, called mifepristone, chemically blocks the naturally occurring hormone progesterone. Blocking progesterone leads to fetal demise by starving the baby of oxygen and nutrients. The second pill, taken within forty-eight hours of the first, called misoprostol, causes a miscarriage by initiating contractions.[2]

The abortion pill was first tested on volunteers in Switzerland in 1982.[3] But it wasn't until 2000 that the US Food and Drug Administration (FDA) approved the use of the chemical mifepristone (also called Mifeprex) found in RU-486 for use by women seeking abortion. The pill regimen ends a pregnancy within seventy days of the woman's last menstrual period.

According to a 2017 Guttmacher study, 39 percent of all abortions in the United States were initiated through the use of the abortion pill regimen, and the numbers continuously increase.[4] Heartbeat International estimates that 50 percent of American abortions will be instigated by these pills within the next year or so.[5]

Reversing Chemical Abortions

Dr. Matt Harrison is a family practitioner in North Carolina. In 2006, he and his colleagues helped pioneer the abortion pill reversal protocol. Through the use of progesterone, Dr. Harrison saved the pregnancy of their first abortion pill reversal client. That child was born healthy in 2007.[6]

Two years later, in California, Dr. George Delgado tested progesterone as a way to save a pregnancy and also found it successful.[7]

Progesterone, a naturally occurring hormone, has been used for more than fifty years to protect pregnancies from naturally occurring miscarriage.[8] In fact, Mary LeQuieu, the former executive director of Care Net of Albuquerque, was saved from an abortion long before Dr. Harrison or Dr. Delgado started researching progesterone.

One of the First Abortion Reversal Survivors Tells Her Story

In an interview in 2019, Mary LeQuieu shared with the authors her incredible story of surviving an attempted abortion. We sat together in her office in Albuquerque just months before she retired after serving twenty years in pro-life ministry. She continues to volunteer within the pro-life movement both at her local PRC and with Care Net.

> I was one of the very first people whose life was saved by the abortion pill reversal.
>
> My mom found her diary from the 1950s and her notes from when she was carrying me. Her doctor's partner told her she was losing me and, if I did survive, that I would be [developmentally disabled], have breathing issues, be physically deformed, and die soon after I was born. His solution was to give [my mom] a series of pills that caused a chemical abortion. We don't know what that was, but we do know that her regular physician, Dr. Brown, came out to her house and gave her a shot of progesterone,

which had just become available, to reverse the effect of the pills. He also prescribed a series of medications and ordered bed rest for her.

Here I am sixty-plus years later. I laugh because his prediction of breathing issues did prove true, but it took sixty-some years to get there.

I know pro-abortion forces hate the concept of abortion pill reversal, and yet we know that over one thousand lives have been saved since they started tracking it.

Look at that number. How many classrooms does one thousand lives fill?

If [pro-choice individuals] really believed in choice, they would support a woman's right to change her mind. But I think that just shows the heart: they're not about choice.

We're about choice.... We give [women who come to us] the information so they can make a choice—an informed choice.

Abortion Pill Reversal Research

Mary LeQuieu's story is unique because her abortion reversal happened before abortion was even legalized. Her doctor understood the basic characteristics of progesterone and tested the theory that it could be used to save a child from a chemical abortion. It worked. Years later, Dr. Harrison and Dr. Delgado tested the same theory and found success as well. Together they began to study progesterone to combat the abortion pill. But studying abortion pill reversal is difficult.

Dr. Delgado founded the Steno Institute, a pro-life research organization that conducts studies on abortion reversal and other pro-life issues. Dr. Delgado and Dr. Harrison joined forces, along with other pro-life doctors, combining their research to showcase the potential to give women a second chance to choose life after initiating a chemical abortion. Dr. Delgado also founded the Abortion Pill Reversal program, which Heartbeat International grafted into their network in 2018, naming it Abortion Pill Rescue (APR). Dr. Delgado and Dr. Harrison serve as medical advisers with Heartbeat International and train their affiliates on APR protocol.

Some oppose abortion pill reversal, though, claiming that there is no good evidence to show that it is successful. To date, there are very few studies on the use of progesterone because abortion providers do not want a reversal available. And pro-life doctors will not test the abortion pill on women as a matter of principle. One study by a pro-abortion doctor did take place, though it was not completed due to health concerns for its participants.

In a 2019 study published in the journal *Obstetrics & Gynecology*, ten women seeking abortions took part in research to discover whether progesterone really worked to stop the effects of mifepristone. All the women in the study took mifepristone to begin a chemical abortion. Five of the women received progesterone treatment daily and the other five women were given a placebo.[9]

The study was stopped after three women were rushed to the hospital. Two of the three women needed emergency surgery because of their extreme hemorrhaging (one of whom needed a blood transfusion). These women were not in the group receiving progesterone. Mifepristone caused the hemorrhaging. (Hemorrhaging is a potential side effect of mifepristone, which is why the FDA places it on their drug Risk Evaluation Mitigation Strategy list.) The other woman taken to the hospital was from the group given progesterone, but she did not require surgery and her bleeding stopped on its own.

Rather than exposing the fact that the abortion pill was to blame for these side effects, the media spun the research to sound as if the abortion reversal treatment was at fault for endangering women. The reality is that 80 percent (four of the five) of those receiving progesterone after taking the abortion pill were healthy and the heartbeats of their babies were detected after two weeks. The news that progesterone kept women from severe hemorrhaging and sustained the lives of their babies was ignored by the Society of Family Planning, the pro-abortion group that funded the research.[10]

Abortion Pill Access, Safety, and Choice

Unbiased research is hard to come by in this area. This is true especially because pro-life researchers would never do a study that involved intentionally giving women the abortion pill. Still, some good data has been emerging to confirm abortion pill reversal. Research done by the Steno Institute shows the positive effects of progesterone on women, though pro-abortion groups ignore their findings. Planned Parenthood's website dismisses pro-life research, stating: "Claims about treatments that reverse the effects of medication abortion are out there.... But these claims haven't been proven in reliable medical studies—nor have they been tested for safety, effectiveness, or the likelihood of side effects."[11]

In their 2018 peer-reviewed study, *A Case Series Detailing the Successful Reversal of the Effects of Mifepristone Using Progesterone*, the Steno Institute found:

- 64% to 68% of the pregnancies were saved through abortion pill reversal
- no increase in birth defects
- a lower preterm delivery rate than the general population[12]

The American Association of Pro-Life Obstetricians and Gynecologists supports abortion pill reversal and has been lobbying for laws requiring women to be informed that abortion reversal could be possible if they regret their decision and seek help within seventy-two hours. They say it is part of a woman's right to "informed consent prior to abortion."[13]

But pro-abortion advocate Guttmacher Institute said, "6 states require medically inaccurate information that a medication abortion can be stopped after the woman takes the first dose of pills."[14]

Another Guttmacher report complains that mifepristone cannot be sold over the counter until the FDA removes it from the Risk Evaluation Mitigation Strategy (REMS) list. The REMS list restricts access to certain drugs and requires doctors to fully disclose all harmful side effects to the patient before giving the prescription. By being on this list, mifepristone can be taken only after a client signs a form stating that she has been counseled on the risks of the pill and what to do if she experiences any harmful symptoms, such as heavy bleeding, abdominal pain, vomiting, or fever.

Due to the number of serious potential complications, the FDA's warning tells the physician that his or her responsibility is to warn the patient and let her know whom to call if she experiences any negative side effects:

> Before prescribing MIFEPREX, inform the patient about the risk of these serious events. Ensure that the patient knows whom to call and what to do, including going to an Emergency Room if none of the provided contacts are reachable, if she experiences sustained fever, severe abdominal pain, prolonged heavy bleeding, or syncope, or if she experiences abdominal pain

> or discomfort, or general malaise (including weak-
> ness, nausea, vomiting, or diarrhea) for more than 24
> hours after taking misoprostol.[15]

Guttmacher claims that the FDA label is "medically unwar-
ranted" and advocates for federal and state laws that allow for access
to the abortion pill regimen without requiring the client to meet with
a licensed physician.

However, more easily accessible abortion pills would eliminate
the medically necessary interaction and counsel vital for a woman to
understand all the risks and side effects of mifepristone. A woman
facing an unplanned pregnancy often already feels isolated. Removing
the REMS warning and label would possibly keep a woman from personal interaction with a doctor who could inform her of the potentially
critical side effects of the drug.

The FDA does not lightly claim that the abortion pill can be
dangerous and should be released only after a client receives all the
information about the risks involved. In fact, the FDA's REMS statement regarding mifepristone admits that "serious and sometimes fatal
infections and bleeding occur very rarely following spontaneous, surgical, and medical abortions, including following MIFEPREX use."[16]

The FDA's guidelines under the Risk Evaluation Mitigation
Strategy exist to ensure that women who take the abortion pill understand the risks and have access to emergency care if they experience
complications associated with a chemical abortion.

If pro-abortion groups truly care about women's health, why
would they fight to remove laws that ensure women understand the
risks their choices could have on their own health?

Dr. Matt Harrison, who helped pioneer abortion pill reversal and
serves as a medical adviser for Heartbeat's APR option line, said:

One thing I think that's interesting is how the abortion industry uses the very rare exceptions to the rule. [They claim] we need abortion to be legal in cases of rape, incest, and life-threatening problems. Those cases do exist, but they are extremely rare in elective abortions. Then they [reject abortion pill reversal treatment], claiming that the number of women who want to reverse their abortion is very low. I would say no woman is insignificant. The fact that [abortion providers] feel like the number of women who want to reverse [a chemical abortion] is insignificant tells me they don't really care about women. They just care about abortion. If they really cared about women and what they want, then they would try to support a woman's desire to reverse her abortion.

Why would pro-abortion organizations desire mifepristone to be accessible over the counter, without any physician oversight, when it can be severely harmful to women? How is easy access to potentially life-threatening pills dubbed "women's health" or "care"? Likewise, in a world that celebrates a woman's right to choose, what happens if she regrets her initial decision? Why would pro-choice groups desire to stop a woman from knowing she still has the opportunity to change her mind and try to save her pregnancy within a certain time frame?

Why Would Anyone Refuse a Woman a Second Chance to Choose?

Just because pro-abortion groups are not researching abortion pill reversal thoroughly does not make it "medically inaccurate." Though the success of chemical abortion reversal varies depending on the age of the fetus and the time progesterone treatment begins after a mother takes the abortion pill, it does have up to a 68 percent chance of working, according to Dr. Delgado's research.[17] We agree with Heartbeat International's statement: "No woman should ever feel forced to finish an abortion she regrets."[18]

If a woman immediately regrets her decision after inducing a chemical abortion, she can call 1-800-712-HELP, the 24-7 Abortion Pill Rescue Network. Heartbeat International has registered nurses across the country who receive calls from Heartbeat's help line. The nurses, who often work in pregnancy resource centers, talk with women, counsel them, and connect them to locations like Centro Tepeyac Women's Center, where they can initiate this lifesaving protocol.

So far, more than a thousand mothers have changed their minds and successfully saved their children from a chemical abortion.[19] One of those mothers is Isabella.

Isabella's Second Chance

Months earlier, when Centro Tepeyac Women's Center began developing their plan to provide for women who rethink their abortion choice, Isabella and Luis were falling in love. They were young and lovestruck as spring semester finished at their high school. They'd been dating for three months when Isabella's birthday came with the shocking news that she was pregnant. Her entire world began to fall apart. She loved Luis but was terrified of the thought of having a baby during her junior year of high school, let alone facing her family with this news.

Taking an abortion pill as quickly as possible seemed to be her only hope for a normal life, but Isabella instantly regretted swallowing that little pill. As it slid down her throat, she began to cry. She really did love children and hoped to be a mom someday. She never thought she would stop a pregnancy, but she also never expected to be pregnant at seventeen. She and Luis rushed out of the abortion clinic. They quickly pulled out their phones and searched "Is it possible to stop a chemical abortion?"

Emotion overtook Isabella; she couldn't even see the online search results. Luis scrolled past the first few links to the abortion clinic's website and found an ad for Abortion Pill Rescue. The individual who answered his call quickly located the nearest APR pregnancy resource center and provided its phone number.

> We regret our first choice of taking the abortion pill, but we are so incredibly thankful for the way you helped us choose [our baby] again.

With tires screeching, Isabella and Luis raced out of the abortion clinic parking lot, headed toward hope. Their hearts beat faster as the landscape seemed to move too slowly, mile after mile. The pregnancy center was only an hour away, but they were all too aware that every minute that passed was crucial to saving their baby's life.

When they finally walked into the pregnancy center, Isabella's and Luis's eyes were glazed with shock, looking like deer caught in headlights. Isabella's hand shook uncontrollably as she filled out the necessary paperwork.

After walking her to an exam room, Kathleen, the center sonographer, saw her jitters and understood the trauma she felt. With a heart overflowing with compassion, Kathleen gently smiled. "You are a brave woman. Let's do a pregnancy test first; then we can provide an ultrasound to see if there is still a heartbeat. We will do everything we can to save your baby, but we don't have much time."

The pregnancy test was still positive. Kathleen slid the ultrasound machine close, and Isabella flinched just slightly at the feeling of the cool gel on her abdomen. Her pulse quickened, and she held her breath, eyes glued to the flickering black-and-white screen.

A nine-week-old baby's small form appeared on the screen. The room was silent as their eyes searched for the little pulses of heartbeat. There they were! The tiny but very clear flashes in the middle of the baby's form drew their attention; the heart was still beating! The tension in the room turned to joy and relief. The baby was alive, wiggling around, safe for now from the devastating effects of the abortion pill.

Another waterfall of tears flowed down Isabella's face—but this time they were tinged with joy. "Our little one is alive!" She smiled and pointed. "Look at that little body!" She and Luis were in awe.

"The baby is alive right now, but it's still a race against time." Kathleen reminded the parents of the precarious reality. Their baby's life was in danger without some kind of intervention.

Kathleen consulted with the clinic's medical director, who immediately sent in a prescription for progesterone in accordance with the APR treatment guidelines.

"You need to take this progesterone regimen to counteract the effects of the first dose of the abortion pill. You're going to have to take progesterone every day for the next week. You may need to continue taking this throughout the rest of your first trimester to secure the safety of your child. This is 68 percent successful, so we cannot guarantee that it will work, but we are here for you and will be here for you no matter what happens. We won't know if it was successful until we perform another ultrasound, so let's schedule one for Monday," the clinic's medical director informed them.

Each day that went by was pure torture for Isabella, Luis, and each one of the staff who assisted with their appointment at the pregnancy center. They prayed, fasted, and called one another to see how things were going. Everyone held their breath for Monday's follow-up.

With urgency similar to the prior week, Isabella and Luis returned to the pregnancy center to find out whether their efforts to save their baby were successful. Isabella felt her own heart pounding in her ears as they again strained to see the rhythmic lines of a little heartbeat on the ultrasound machine.

This time a ten-week-old baby's body appeared! The rhythmic flashes of the tiny heartbeat punctuated the screen, like music notes of a unique song. The child was alive and growing normally! Erupting with laughter, they shared their joy together.

"Our baby's alive!" They embraced each other with sincere relief and cried, "It worked! The pills you gave us worked!"

"Thank you for giving us a second chance to choose life," Luis said when he picked up baby supplies a few months later in preparation for the arrival of their little boy. He continued, "We regret our first choice of taking the abortion pill, but we are so incredibly thankful for the way you helped us choose him again. Each of you is a gift from God to us. We were hopeless and helpless, and you didn't just save one life; you saved our family. Thank you!"

On February 23, 2018, Isabella gave birth to her son. They took a family photo, adding the words "Life is a gift from God" to the image, and sent it to the staff at Centro Tepeyac. The framed picture hangs in the pregnancy center's staff room, a daily reminder of how fragile, beautiful, and wonderful life is.

> We were hopeless and helpless,
> and you didn't just save one life;
> you saved our family.

Wondering Where to Start?

If abortion pill reversal is new to you, you're not alone. The vast majority of people outside pregnancy resource clinics are unaware of the possibility of reversing a chemical abortion.

Educate yourself more about abortion pill reversal at Pregnancy Help News (www.pregnancyhelpnews.com) and Abortion Pill Rescue (www.abortionpillreversal.com).

You can help spread the word by talking about abortion pill reversal. Inform those around you by winsomely opening the conversation about the use of progesterone to preserve life when a mother changes her mind.

Inform your pastor about the resources cited above, and see how your church could help inform your community about abortion pill reversal. People in your church may know of individuals who need this information. Continue advocating for life, and bring awareness of the resources you're learning about. Your church could place information about abortion pill reversal and other pregnancy resources on your bulletin board or provide shareable cards to give to others who may need that resource. Remember that there is always hope. Those who are in an abortion clinic's parking lot are not doomed. Be ready to inform them of the hope that exists to reverse a chemical abortion and to find healing in Christ for irreversible choices.

Consider asking your friends:

- "Have you heard about the recent studies by both pro-choice and pro-life groups that reveal progesterone's ability to protect the lives of the mother and child after the abortion pill is ingested?" Challenge your friends to

remain informed about current issues and advances in
women's health.

- "Do you think physicians prescribing the abortion pill
should inform women about risks associated with it and
the potential to reverse it before they take it?"

- "Why would giving women a second chance to choose
be a negative thing? Why don't more women know
about the potential for abortion pill reversal?"

Reflecting the Father's Heart

Hosea 4:6 reveals the broken heart of God in the face of limited
truth and the abuse of power: "My people are destroyed from lack of
knowledge."

We are called to have the same compassion that Jesus exemplifies
and God reveals throughout Scripture. His heart is for life: "For I
take no pleasure in the death of anyone, declares the Sovereign LORD.
Repent and live!" (Ezek. 18:32).

Scripture provides hope for true freedom no matter what our past
may include. As Jesus said in John 8:32, "Then you will know the
truth, and the truth will set you free."

The fact that a woman has the chance to turn away from her first
choice and choose life instead is profound. God invites us all to turn
away from destruction to life; that's what the gospel is all about. We
cannot look down on a woman who may have initially chosen to ingest
an abortion pill, because each one of us has taken on some toxic form
of sin and is in need of hope, salvation, and healing.

No matter your story, consider the fact that God "is close to the
brokenhearted and saves those who are crushed in spirit" (Ps. 34:18).

Prayer

Father of all comfort and hope, author of forgiveness and abundant life, and restorer of all things, help me to reflect Your extravagant compassion for those experiencing the pain or regret of abortion. Help me spread the message about how lives can be saved. Please give me opportunities to raise awareness about abortion pill reversal, and help me engage in winsome conversations about Your heart for women, men, and unborn babies. Help me to be bold—bold to admit mistakes and take action. Thank You that You're a God who enters into our lives and brings hope even when it seems too late. Heal me from my own pain and brokenness, and restore me so I can be an agent of Your healing in my home, my church, and my community. Amen.

Chapter 10

Healing after Abortion

Life and Forgiveness after Abortion

"When I faced my unplanned pregnancy, no one gave me information; nobody shared with me the risk of abortion. I had no idea. I was clueless. I can never go back and undo the decision I was pressured into when I was twenty-one. The only thing I can do is receive what God has for me from that. This is why I'm a believer today. I walked through that very painful, sorrowful experience, and I realized how desperately I needed God. But on the other side, He has used my story to help many women choose life. To help many women who are struggling with a past abortion choice to come to a place where they can find God's forgiveness and healing."

Mary LeQuieu, former executive director of Care Net
of Albuquerque and chemical abortion survivor

"For over twenty-seven years, this was a story I felt like I should bury," Pam Daugherty said to a room full of people at a PRC banquet in Waller, Texas. "But we all have a story, and I want to tell you mine."

She continued, her voice full of resolve: "When I was seventeen years old, I decided to have sex with my high school boyfriend. My mom was open about sex and encouraged me to at least wait until I was in love."

Pam took her mom's advice to heart. She had been dating her boyfriend, Brad, for three years, and she knew she was in love. She felt like the time was right. But as soon as they had sex, Brad broke up with her. His reasoning? His dad told him that good girls wait.

Pam was devastated and confused. She had no idea how to process the feelings of hurt and shame and the belief that what had happened was somehow her fault.

"Weeks later, after Brad broke my heart, I missed my period. I was moody, and I felt sick. Consequently, I decided to take a pregnancy test," Pam recounted. "I remember I went to the store with my friend and we did the pregnancy test in the restroom of a fast-food restaurant."

When the two lines appeared, she broke down.

"I was terrified to look like 'that girl.' We went to church regularly; how could I ruin my parents' reputation?" she said.

Scared, confused, and feeling completely alone, she had no idea what to do. She called Brad and tearfully told him what had happened.

"Brad kept telling me that I did it on purpose and that it wouldn't work. He was going to school next year to be a dentist. I was going to be responsible for ruining his life," she explained. "He told me that the abortion clinic was where you went for an unplanned pregnancy. They would handle everything."

The doctors at the clinic told her the pregnancy was so early that it wasn't really a baby yet; it was just cells. Since she was underage, she technically needed parental consent to have the abortion. Brad's solution to the problem was to steal the ID of an older woman for Pam to use.

"Brad went with me, and he sat with me and held my hand as I bawled on the table," she said.

After the procedure, the doctor, who was aware of the fake ID, told Pam she could never tell anyone about the abortion because she was underage. For years she kept it a secret.

"The memory of the child I never fought for lived in my head," Pam said. "The milestones I was missing from that baby's life. Not knowing if that baby was a boy or girl haunted me. I asked, *Why? Why couldn't an adult have spoken truth to me?*"

Years later, Pam was asked to be a chaperone at a youth retreat for her church. When she arrived at the retreat, the sermon was about how Satan uses your sin to stop you from doing what God wants you to do. That the worst things you've done in life can still be used to glorify God and help others heal. The message hit her like a ton of bricks. She knew immediately that God wanted her to start talking about what had happened to her all those years ago, that her story could help other girls who might be in a similar situation.

That very night, Pam shared her story with the youth group for the first time.

"I needed to tell people about the hurt you live with after choosing abortion," she said. "I wanted to find a way for girls to hear the things that I didn't."

Since that moment, God has used Pam in ways she never could have imagined. She received a call right after the retreat asking her if she'd like to interview for a job at a pro-life organization where she could work with pregnancy centers to reach more girls like her—teens who are unexpectedly pregnant and considering abortion.

"God has given me amazing opportunities," she said. "I prayed for a way to be able to reach young girls like me and to connect them with the women from pregnancy centers who could help them at this critical moment in their lives."

Sharing the Problem Creates Solutions

The biggest turning point in Pam's story was when she started sharing her message of hope and redemption. She broke the silence and spoke.

So many women live with shame and regret from past abortions and have never told anyone about them. One major reason for their silence is that the church isn't talking about abortion or offering opportunities for healing after abortion.

Many pastors aren't sharing the message of forgiveness—specifically for abortion—from the pulpit. This omission reinforces the shame that many women and men feel along with the lie that those facing an unplanned pregnancy can't get the help they need from the church.

Brenda Shuler is the vice president of services at a pregnancy resource center in Colorado. For more than fifteen years, Brenda has also run Bridges of Hope, an after-abortion recovery program at her PRC. One of the most common themes she sees in her work with women who have had abortions is a belief that forgiveness doesn't apply to them.

"They see abortion as something they don't believe God can forgive. They struggle to release it. There is an isolation that runs through this thinking, because they start to believe they are the only ones who have had an abortion. Many women in the Christian community feel they cannot talk about it because people would think less of them," Shuler explained.

In 2016, Care Net released a study on abortion and the church with LifeWay Research. Among American women who'd had an abortion and attended a Christian church once a month or more at the time of the study, 52 percent said no one at church knew they had terminated a pregnancy. Additionally, 49 percent of women who had had an abortion agreed that pastors' teachings on forgiveness didn't seem to apply to terminated pregnancies, and only four in ten women who'd had an abortion thought it was safe to talk with a pastor about abortion.[1]

"Shame and guilt run deep," Shuler said. "There is a common misconception that they don't believe they have the right to grieve because it was their choice. They feel they have no value or right to forgiveness because of their past actions."

Sadly, on top of the guilt and shame they feel, many women who have had abortions don't believe that the church is a safe place to talk about their experiences. They have largely negative feelings about how they will be viewed by those in the congregation. In fact, 64 percent think they are more likely to be gossiped about than helped by churchgoers.[2]

The fact is, our churches are filled with sinful people who find redemption in Christ. Rather than gossiping about a woman facing an unplanned pregnancy, the church needs to express God's love, forgiveness, grace, and redemption. Still, those who do not feel safe talking about their past or current struggles can feel isolated and judged even though their sins are no less forgivable by God than another's.

"The church has to be talking about how to care for women after an abortion," Shuler said. "By not speaking on the topic, they are reinforcing the isolation women feel in the church."

Pam echoed this. She believes that the more women who've experienced abortion share their stories in the church, the more power they have to help other women.

"Use all that emotion to help others," she said. "You can do this by sharing your story, one person at a time, by talking about choosing abortion. Talk about how it changed your life. Be the voice for those who need help. Let God use your story to help make abortion unthinkable."

> Women [and men] in the church need to know that [abortion] is an issue worth addressing and it is a wound worth healing.

Will They Kick Me Out?

When Victoria Robinson was in her twenties, she had an abortion. The doctor told her that she wasn't very far along—just six to eight weeks—and that her baby was just "a clump of tissue" at that point. No harm, no foul.

Fast-forward ten years, and she is a worship leader at her church with four young daughters.

"I led worship thinking, *If* abortion *was tattooed on my forehead, would they kick me off of this stage? Would they even let me sing these songs?* I was terrified of them knowing my secret," she said.

Her memories and the topic of abortion kept appearing in her life. For three years, the director of the local PRC, Annie, who happened to attend the same church as Victoria, kept trying to get her to volunteer with them. Victoria noticed that every time she would lead worship at a women's conference, someone would come up to her after and tell her a story of having an abortion: pastors' wives, doctors' wives, judges, women from all backgrounds.

"I'd pray with them, and then I would cry out to God and ask why He wasn't helping me," she said.

Then one day it all shifted for her. A woman came up to Victoria and asked for prayer because she was still broken from an abortion she'd had twenty-seven years before.

"I saw her healed in that moment, and somehow that was it for me," she said. "I called Annie after that and told her I was ready to come volunteer."

Victoria was going through the volunteer training at the pregnancy center when one day, she and the other volunteers were looking at a model of the embryonic development of a baby.

"I looked at the stage for six to eight weeks, and it took everything in me not to break down," she said.

Victoria went home and sat sobbing in her car for two hours. She was in her car for so long that her daughter came out to check on her.

"Mommy, what's wrong? Did someone die?" her daughter asked.

For years Victoria had convinced herself that if she told the people she loved most she'd had an abortion, they would hate her. But in that moment, she told her daughter the truth.

"My beautiful daughter held me and said, 'Mommy, Jesus forgives you, and I forgive you. You're such a good mom.' The grace and mercy she showed me were the same I felt Christ showed me," she said.

Victoria finally had a breakthrough.

"So I went to Annie, and I told her I had an abortion, and she said, 'I know. I've been waiting for you to tell me. Now we're going to get you into after-abortion counseling, and God is going to redeem your life.'"

Not long after they talked, Victoria went through an abortion-recovery class at Annie's PRC, and it changed everything for her.

"Now I conduct and teach those same abortion-recovery retreats for women like me—to remind them that there is life after abortion," Victoria said. "I want women everywhere to know that God forgives after an abortion."

After-Abortion Counseling and the Church

These stories and statistics point to a serious issue: the majority of women facing an unplanned pregnancy don't see the church as a safe or welcoming place to help them in their situation. And those who have had an abortion are often not getting the help and healing they need. The church is failing women in this arena.

The same Care Net study referenced earlier found that 51 percent of women said that they were not aware if churches have a ministry prepared to discuss options during an unplanned pregnancy.[3]

"Women [and men] in the church need to know that [abortion] is an issue worth addressing and it is a wound worth healing," Brenda Shuler said.

Conversations in the Church

The first step to improving, or beginning, conversations in the church is connecting with a local pregnancy resource center. This should be one of the first places pastors and other church leaders look for resources to address unplanned pregnancies and to reach women in their congregations who've had abortions.

The Care Net study found that only 5 percent of women were referred to a local PRC by their church. Your church can help improve this number by simply sharing the information and introducing the topic to your congregation. Pregnancy centers can help pastors find the language and tools to start talking about unplanned pregnancy, abortion, and after-abortion healing.

It's important to have a nonjudgmental attitude and an honest, compassionate approach with these topics. (Actually, this posture is one our hurting culture is aching to encounter from Christians in many areas.) When intellectually and emotionally equipped in this sensitive topic, pastors will be better able to engage with distressed women and assure them that God forgives abortion. And this should be done in love.

"We have to be careful as pro-life people how we handle those who are already wounded. Don't shoot the wounded. Be very mindful of those who are in pain from their past choices. Many individuals with abortion in their past avoid Mother's Day, Father's

Day, or Sanctity of Human Life Sunday each January. Keep in mind that many in the congregation have experienced [abortion] and it is their story. They can feel shame, guilt, pain, and isolation," Shuler said.

> We have to be careful as pro-life people how we handle those who are already wounded.

Another way the local church can approach this conversation is to initiate small groups or one-on-one mentoring to discuss after-abortion healing. Additionally, your church can invite someone from your local PRC to speak on the issue and start raising awareness. Normalizing the topic will equip everyone in the congregation to engage in grace-filled conversations as they arise. But realize it takes time to build trust and a culture where individuals feel safe to admit their deepest and most closely kept secrets. Don't be discouraged if people do not initially respond to your offer. Keep providing the resources, and pray that God will bring people to you for healing.

The church should also consider displaying the number to a local pregnancy center in a frequently visited area of the church or sharing it on its website. Also explain how PRCs can refer women to counseling groups. Shuler's pregnancy center hosts a Bible study and counseling group for women who have experienced abortion.

It is worth noting that not just women are affected by abortion.

"There are a lot of men who found out about a pregnancy and they wanted that baby, but their partner had an abortion anyway. He is left to deal with that grief," Shuler noted.

The more the church talks about this subject, the more we can start to connect men and women who've experienced abortion to hope and healing.

> The Lord ... has been grieving with you—
> grieving that you keep hurting. He is wishing
> that you could see what He sees in you.

"Encourage people that it doesn't matter how long ago it was," Shuler went on to say. "This wound doesn't heal on its own; it needs to be addressed directly and not swept away as if it's nothing. Abortion has deep and lasting effects, and it affects other parts of our relationships and personality. We don't even realize how connected it is to every other part of our identity."

Pam, the woman from earlier in the chapter, believes that finding healing is the most important thing a woman or man can do after an abortion, especially when it comes to restoring his or her identity.

"Talk with the Lord about your grief," she said. "He has been grieving with you—grieving that you keep hurting. He is wishing that you could see what He sees in you."

She added, "Go through an abortion recovery program. Allow God to show you how you can use the memory of your child to glorify Him and to help other women."

Wondering Where to Start?

Check in with your local PRC to learn about their after-abortion programs. Many offer in-depth Bible studies, groups, or counseling—sometimes all three. Brenda Shuler recommends the following studies for individuals after abortion but notes that this issue should be taught in conjunction with trained staff.

- *Forgiven and Set Free: A Post-Abortion Bible Study for Women* by Linda Cochrane

- *Surrendering the Secret: Healing the Heartbreak of Abortion* by Pat Layton
- *Her Choice to Heal: Finding Spiritual and Emotional Peace after Abortion* by Sydna Massé
- *Healing a Father's Heart: A Post-Abortion Bible Study for Men* by Linda Cochrane and Kathy Jones

Additionally, AbAnon (Abortion Anonymous at www.abanon .org) is an online resource for individuals to access studies, groups, or online videos and classes to help them work through their healing journey from the comfort of their own homes.

Reflecting the Father's Heart

The Psalms hold the full gamut of emotional expression—from joy and praise to sorrow and deep pain. Hope weaves its way through these songs because the writers knew that God is present even when human emotions tell us He isn't. To those who are in pain and feel loss, Psalm 147:3 says that God "heals the brokenhearted and binds up their wounds."

God's promise of heart healing is throughout Scripture, but here are a few examples:

> Come to me, all you who are weary and burdened, and I will give you rest. Take my yoke upon you and learn from me, for I am gentle and humble in heart, and you will find rest for your souls. (Matt. 11:28–29)

> "He himself bore our sins" in his body on the cross, so that we might die to sins and live for righteousness; "by his wounds you have been healed." (1 Pet. 2:24)

"'He will wipe every tear from their eyes. There will be no more death' or mourning or crying or pain, for the old order of things has passed away."

He who was seated on the throne said, "I am making everything new!" Then he said, "Write this down, for these words are trustworthy and true." (Rev. 21:4–5)

If you have abortion in your story, don't allow the Enemy to devalue you and keep you from accepting the gift of God's forgiveness. Jesus died so that we would have life in abundance, and the Enemy does his best to keep us from that. God's forgiveness is greater than your sin.

Whether or not abortion is in your past, you can participate in God's redemptive story by compassionately loving those who need healing. Read the words to Keith and Kristyn Getty's "Compassion Hymn."[4]

We stood beneath the cross of Calvary
And gazed on Your face
At the thorns of oppression
And the wounds of disgrace,
For surely You have borne our suffering
And carried our grief
As You pardoned the scoffer
And showed grace to the thief.

How beautiful the feet that carry
This gospel of peace
To the fields of injustice
And the valleys of need—

> *To be a voice of hope and healing,*
> *To answer the cries*
> *Of the hungry and helpless*
> *With the mercy of Christ.*

Prayer

Dear Father, help me be a voice of hope and healing to the men and women around me who are hurting from a past abortion. God, I ask You to heal my own heart in the areas where it is still broken. Transform my heart to reflect a deeper, truer, more vibrant expression of Your compassion for those who are wounded, including myself. Help me remember how big You are, how deeply You love me and those around me. Remind me of the limitless forgiveness You express to those who turn to You. Thank You for being loving and good beyond my comprehension. Thank You for providing redemption for all, and show me how to participate in Your work in my home, church, and community. Amen.

Section 4

Taking Action

How You and Your Church
Can Make a Life-Changing,
Lifesaving Difference

Chapter 11

Church Participation in the Pro-Life Movement

How the Church Can Participate in Pro-Life Work

What does the gospel have to do with women's reproductive health?

What right does Christianity have to project its morality onto anyone?

How dare followers of Christ tell others what they can and cannot do with their bodies?

Life is complicated and nuanced. The factors that influence major decisions are complex and often weighted. So how does the gospel interact with life? How can the faith community answer the questions posed by culture?

The attitudes and questions of our society have, unfortunately, quieted the voice of the evangelical church in recent decades. With moral relativism increasing, those who should speak up for the vulnerable have proportionately decreased their engagement on pro-life topics. As we've peeled back the many layers in this book, we've explored how the church can meaningfully engage individuals in their congregations and communities.

Many Christians avoid pro-life topics for a myriad of reasons, some fiercely political, some deeply personal. We hope we've destigmatized the issue along the way. But as we wrap up, we would like to summarize how we, as the church, can be involved and bring fresh energy to engage the pro-life narrative in loving ways that will save and change lives forever.

Sobering Stats

In the spring of 2019, only 4 percent out of fifty thousand sermons delivered at six thousand US churches addressed the topic of abortion.[1]

Care Net released the following stats revealing how individuals who had an abortion interact with the church:

- More than one in three women were attending a Christian church at least once a month when they had their first abortion.
- Half of women agree that churches do not have a ministry prepared to discuss options during an unplanned pregnancy.
- 65% of women believe that church members judge expectant single women.
- Half of women don't feel that sermons on God's forgiveness apply to their abortions.[2]

When the church doesn't engage the issue of human life, its silence screams. The silence gives implied permission for abortion, or worse yet, the church's silence can give the impression that the gospel has nothing to say to someone facing an unplanned pregnancy.

The politics, pain, and passionate tension surrounding the topic of abortion cause those with words of life to avoid this particularly painful topic. But in avoiding the discomfort of sensitive memories or hard subjects simply because they are politically charged, the church also misses opportunities to introduce healing to hurting hearts.

The tragedy of a quiet church is the missed opportunities to tell the abundantly rich, beautiful, healing, and inspiring story of the gospel: A story that provides the foundation for the value of every human life, no matter its stage of development. A story that reveals a God who champions the vulnerable, cherishes the outcast, and heals the wounded. This is the story given uniquely through Scripture, and it is our responsibility as the church to not only tell it but also live it as a daily expression of God's kingdom invading and redefining the world through us.

What Is Our Story?

Scripture does not portray a God who rejects the weak, the poor, the oppressed, or the sinful. The entire narrative reveals a God who loves lavishly, forgives freely, and heals holistically.

Our story begins with the intentional design of male and female in Genesis 1, with the very breath of God animating the human body in Genesis 2. Life's spark and sustainability are both gifts from God. The design of humanity includes sexuality created to be enjoyed in obedience to the mandate to be fruitful and multiply. But those who read Genesis will notice that it didn't take long before sin ravaged the world with violence, oppression, and unrestricted selfishness.

Through the story of Scripture, we discover a number of vulnerable women and observe how God cared for them. Judah's family ostracized his Canaanite daughter-in-law after she was widowed in Genesis 38. The family hampered her right to have a child until she tricked her father-in-law, Judah, into sleeping with her. As strange as the story is, Tamar was justified for upholding her right to have a child, and one of the twins born to her is listed in Jesus' ancestry.

Additionally, Rahab, a Canaanite prostitute, was saved from destruction in Jericho because of her faith and the support she gave to Israel's spies (Josh. 2). Her son, Boaz, owned fields where Ruth, the Moabite widow, gleaned. Through their marriage, Ruth received the joy of becoming part of Boaz's family and joined the lineage of the Redeemer of the world. Matthew's genealogy of Jesus includes these women along with Bathsheba and Mary, who both experienced the difficulties of unplanned pregnancies (Matt. 1).

Jesus doesn't just identify with the vulnerable woman; she is also part of His DNA. He not only cares about those with hard, painful, or questionable sexual pasts, but He also carries a part of them in His own blood.

Why We Care

God calls us, as followers of Christ, to represent His heart for the world.

Ignoring the issue of abortion out of discomfort—or deeming the topic too political or polarizing—does not justify our silence. The church needs to stand up for what is at the very heart of the heavenly Father. The One who creates and sustains all life transcended the perceived boundary of heaven and earth to replace decay, brokenness, pain, and sin with His wholeness, healing, and a life lived to the full (see John 10:10).

Scripture describes God intentionally knitting children together in their mothers' wombs (see Ps. 139:13–14). Life is sacred, and inspires wonder and awe. Yet because of our broken world, life is not as it should be. There is pain, disease, circumstantial difficulties, violence, sin, and death. The very core of the gospel shows a God who enters into the messiness of our human lives and begins restoring all things through the life He provides by His death. The church is designed to be God's agent of restoration. We need to care about all the ways sin has broken the world, but nothing is more vital than protecting the life of a human being made in God's image.

Yes, pro-life advocates tend to focus on the little life that has no voice yet. But we must also realize that the parents need the beautiful story of the gospel to touch them too. When God's forgiveness, love, and redemption flood a heart, it heals and restores the past, bringing comfort and empowering the person's future.

As you've seen throughout these stories, making a choice for life is probably more complicated than one might initially think. We must also recognize the fact that life is not easy no matter what a parent chooses.

Life is beautiful. Life is hard. Life is messy.

Grace in the Church

Throughout this book and this chapter specifically, we call the church *up*—not *out*. It's not our goal to shame anyone for not doing enough; you may already be involved in pro-life ministries, and we cheer you on. Nor would we ever shame anyone for his or her past; you're not alone. Compassion is the theme here. Compassion is "sympathetic consciousness of others' distress together with a desire to alleviate it."[3] This is our heart.

Jesus looked with compassion at the masses surrounding Him because they were suffering from their own helplessness (see Matt. 9:36). We all have been lost at one point or another and deeply in need of the Lord's grace, forgiveness, and love to draw us in. Jesus commissioned the church to be His representative, and for that reason our responsibility as believers is to love as He loved and see people as He sees them. To reflect Christ well, we must have compassion for the hurting, the weary, and the lost and provide an introduction to the hope, healing, and rest that can be found only in Him.

Local churches can open their doors to women and men in unplanned pregnancies by surrounding them with the grace-filled community and love found only in Christ. As we've discussed throughout this book, partnerships between PRCs and churches are vitally important. The church can go a step beyond just alleviating economic stress by providing discipleship, community, family, and a support system to individuals who desperately need it.

> Pregnancy resource centers are
> the first response team, and
> the church is the hospital.

There are more than 2,800 pregnancy resource centers around the nation[4] and an estimated 350,000 churches.[5] If every church in the United States partnered with one pregnancy resource center, the PRC would have more than enough volunteers and resources to sustain their lifesaving work.

Organizations like Embrace Grace are working to make partnerships between PRCs and churches a reality. This national nonprofit founded by Amy Ford partners with churches to create support groups for women facing unplanned pregnancies and for those who've had abortions. Serving as a bridge, Embrace Grace takes a three-pronged approach to helping the church reach women:

> **Embrace Grace:** A twelve-week course led by church members, many of whom have had an abortion or have experienced an unplanned pregnancy. This course includes curated curriculum, videos, handouts, and digital resources for leaders. Church members also throw a baby shower for the women midway through the course.

Embrace Life: A twenty-two-week support group where single moms are mentored by women in the church in order to gain new life skills related to parenting, financial stewardship, time management, dating, and many other topics.

Love Boxes: These boxes are filled with gifts: a personal invitation to a church-hosted support group, stories from both a parenting mom and a birth mom, a letter of hope, a journal, and more.

"We've noticed a lot of churches don't know what a PRC is," Ford said.

This is what motivates her to do the work she does. She likes to quote Tony Evans, who said, "Pregnancy centers are the first response team, and the church is the hospital."[6]

"This is a great picture of us all working together," Ford said. "We can make a big difference partnering together with the church."

Embracing Women in Unplanned Pregnancies and Beyond

The mission of Embrace Grace originated from the personal story of Amy Ford, who grew up in the church and had an unplanned pregnancy at nineteen. Her pregnancy felt more difficult because everyone knew she was pregnant but no one talked about it. It was the elephant in the room, making her feel isolated and confused.

"People [at church] didn't know how to talk to me. I felt alone in the crowd, so I just stopped going," she said. "I needed the church at that time, but the church didn't talk about [my pregnancy], so I felt like I wasn't supposed to talk about it either."

Ten years later, leadership at Ford's new church offered her the opportunity to start a group helping other single moms facing unplanned pregnancies. Three women from the community participated in her first group. They studied a book on grace, and they talked about adoption, parenting, and different life skills.

"We saw all three girls transform; they were empowered as women to be the moms God created them to be," Ford said. More women wanted the class, so she taught it again. Then churches started calling, seeking a resource to start similar classes for women in need.

"We realized God wanted us to equip the church to be the church in this area," Ford said. "We had to change the mindset that pregnancy is a sin. Instead, we're helping people heal."

Like Ford, women who find themselves facing unplanned pregnancies feel broken, fearful, anxious, and lacking in answers to handle their circumstances. As we've seen in so many stories, alleviating economic stress and caring for the person physically, emotionally, and spiritually opens a door to a better life.

Authentically Sharing the Gospel and Embracing the Mess

What is your church's current pro-life outreach? How would you describe your church's culture when the hurting (those facing unplanned pregnancies or involved in unhealthy relationships) seek refuge? Judgmental or welcoming? Shaming or blessing?

We, as the body of Christ, must speak truth about God's abundant life. If we don't, who will? Those who need the message most are not those who have their lives together but those who are fractured by sin. As Luke 19:10 states, "The Son of Man came to seek and to save the lost."

When the religious elite of Israel questioned Jesus for associating with broken, sinful people, Jesus responded, "It is not the healthy who need a doctor, but the sick. But go and learn what this means: 'I desire mercy, not sacrifice.' For I have not come to call the righteous, but sinners" (Matt. 9:12–13).

You and your church could be a bridge for individuals to experience God's gracious embrace, forgiveness, healing, and love for the first time. But are you willing to embrace the messiness that comes with doing the hard work of loving like Jesus? Jesus gave this call to His followers, "Go and make disciples of all nations" (Matt. 28:19), knowing that difficulty, sacrifice, frustration, heartache, pain, and loss would be associated with His mandate.

Discipleship is difficult.

Still, discipleship changes lives and hearts. Discipleship is how true and lasting transformation happens in a person. When people are transformed, culture is transformed.

- How would someone find hope and healing at your church?
- In what ways does your church welcome those who are broken and hurting?

> It is by *seeing* the cross and the community beneath it that [people] come to believe in God.
>
> —Dietrich Bonhoeffer[7]

Caring for Abortion-Vulnerable Men and Women within Your Church

It may be hard to believe, or it may be easier to simply ignore the fact, that we interact with individuals who are abortion vulnerable or who've had abortions *every day* without even knowing it. She's your favorite teen who watches your children for you on the weekends. He's the youth leader who cheers on your students to succeed. She's your best friend whom you've known for years but who doesn't like to talk about her "crazy college days." Or it could be the quiet older couple who passes out bulletins. They each have a story.

Our world and our churches are filled with limitlessly valuable human beings who need the hope of the gospel.

"Any young person is abortion vulnerable," said Rob Denler, a former youth pastor who is now the men's program director for Alternatives Pregnancy Center in Denver, Colorado.

Young people who get involved in intimate relationships may feel even more pressured to hide an unplanned pregnancy from the church because they fear shame and judgment from their friends and family. Their own circumstances give them more shame than they've ever felt without additional voices chiming in. You just don't know how difficult it might be to choose life until you're faced with that decision.

"It's easy to be pro-life when you're not experiencing an unexpected pregnancy in a crisis situation," Denler continued. "It's easy when it's someone else's deal. But when we experience it ourselves, that's when we have to come to terms with what we truly believe about life."

> Let's be the body of Christ, embracing and celebrating life as it is and fostering a thriving environment for life to become what it should be.

How can we be authentic in our faith while embracing people where they are, as they are? How can we introduce them to the transformative power of the gospel?

Consider the demographics of your church, and ask yourself these questions:

- Are there many single-parent homes?
- How is your church supporting those families?
- Are there men willing to be surrogate fathers to young men without a fatherly influence, who can teach them how to be godly men?
- Are there individuals willing to come alongside single moms and help them with practical and emotional needs?
- Does your church create a culture of family for those who feel alone and without support?
- If someone found herself in an unplanned pregnancy outside of marriage, would she feel God's love for her at your church, or would shame, judgment, and guilt drive her away?
- What is your church doing to help men and women navigate their choices or find healing from the pain of their past decisions?
- What do you think when you see a woman sitting alone with a fussy baby at church?

Amy Ford offers ideas about practical ways your church can engage with abortion-vulnerable women:

- Watch Facebook's buy/sell/trade pages, and reach out to those seeking help for baby supplies. Invite them to your church.
- Ask God, "How can I be Jesus to someone today?" Some women ask God for a sign; you could be that sign

and the answer to someone's prayer. Your obedience to
the Spirit's guidance could save a life.

- PRAY! Ask God to open the eyes of your heart. Seek to
be used by the Lord as a catalyst to change hearts and
minds for life.

Rob Denler suggests the following ways to engage with abortion-vulnerable men within the church:

- Seek to understand what men are feeling when it comes
to unplanned pregnancy. You can familiarize your-self with the issue online at the National Fatherhood
Initiative (www.fatherhood.org).
- Stop the stigma. Talk about the reality of unplanned
pregnancy. Be honest, kind, real, and loving while offer-ing men a place to discuss their own struggles.
- Inform men—both young and old—about local preg-nancy resource centers and the services they provide.
- Encourage men to talk about the realities of fatherhood—
both good and bad. Being informed removes the mystery
and fear.
- Men who are willing to share their time and stories
make great mentors and coaches for other men.

Church Engagement with Pro-Life Matters

It should be apparent by now how complex and difficult unplanned
pregnancies are. But no matter how a life begins, God reveals Himself
throughout Scripture as one who loves life at every stage, whose heart
breaks at injustice, and who desires restoration. Therefore, we must

speak out. How can you get your church to start talking about the value of all life?

From the pulpit: The same Pew Research study referenced earlier in the chapter found that only 1 percent of fifty thousand sermons gave more than 250 words to the topic of abortion.[8] Many pastors feel pro-life topics have become political in recent years, so it's understandable why they often avoid addressing the issues from the pulpit. Pastors already have a lot on their plates, and the drama they could provoke by bringing up such a seemingly polarizing issue might be daunting. Still, the church is to be a reflection of the Father's heart. Pray for your pastor and encourage him or her. When spoken with love, compassion, and truth, God's Word brings healing and wholeness for anyone.

Include men: Few studies have been done on the effects of abortion on men because culture ostracizes them from the conversation. Catherine T. Coyle's study, *Men and Abortion: A Review of Empirical Reports concerning the Impact of Abortion on Men*, notes that many men struggle after an abortion and don't know how to cope:

> As members of a society which restricts the discussion
> of abortion as a woman's right, post-abortion men
> may be confused by their reactions, unsure of their
> roles or responsibilities, and unlikely to seek help.[9]

Another study by Coyle found that men whose partners had an abortion reported, "in varying degrees, the following as a consequence of their abortion experience: frequent thoughts about the lost child, difficulty concentrating, anger, anxiety, grief, guilt, helplessness, relationship problems, and confusion about the man's role in society."[10]

Men and women have a right to feel the pain of their past. The church has the call to be a voice of hope and healing for both parents.

Congregation Involvement
Training

Reframe your pro-life perspective from political to personal outreach.

- Care Net's *Making Life Disciples* is designed to equip the church to engage in conversations about life and abortion.
- Sidewalk Advocates for Life offers training for those who are called to stand outside abortion clinics and offer judgment-free, loving conversations with women and men who approach the clinics.
- Life Training Institute offers in-person and online trainings to help individuals and groups better understand how to articulate and defend their pro-life views within the marketplace of ideas.
- Find additional resources online at the National Fatherhood Initiative (www.fatherhood.org), Care Net (www.care-net.org), Heartbeat International (www.heartbeatinternational.org), and Save the Storks (www.savethestorks.com).

Connection

Be the bridge to your community by pointing them toward Christ.

- Find your local PRC, and discover how you can partner with them. Invite them to your church to inform your congregation of their services and volunteer opportunities.
- Create a mentoring program for women and men to invest personally in the lives of younger women and

men. People crave meaningful work, and this pairs those who long to serve and share the gospel with those who need relationship.

- Present young men and women with truth about healthy relational boundaries and God's design for marriage and family.

- Offer your church as a safe place for men and women who are vulnerable to abortion so they might experience a supportive family structure.

- Provide those with abortion in their past a place to tell their stories. By sharing, men and women not only heal but also empower others to seek healing and feel safe sharing their stories.

Acknowledge that women [and men] have gone through abortion. Remind them that God can still use them and wants to heal them. As Revelation 12:11 states, we overcome the Enemy "by the blood of the Lamb and by the word of [our] testimony."

—Amy Ford

Support

Offer ongoing spiritual, emotional, and practical care and resources for single-parent and blended families.

- Fix a single mom's car, teach résumé writing, provide access to computers, or provide budgeting advice, financial strategies, or tutoring to parents or their children.

> If the church came alongside single moms and dads and helped them in their time of need, sickness, struggle, etc., we could help make abortion unthinkable. We could show that we actually care for people.
>
> —Rob Denler

- Offer heart-healing classes to help both men and women in the areas of mom wounds, dad wounds, boundaries, dating, soul ties, breaking generational patterns, replacing lies with the truth, forgiveness, and other emotional needs.

> When [men and women] find freedom from the baggage of the past, then they can thrive in their future.
>
> —Amy Ford

Counseling and Mentorship

Open the conversation. Validate the right of both women and men to feel the pain of a lost pregnancy while offering the truth of God's restorative forgiveness, grace, and love.

Give people options of where to get healing. After healing happens, raise up those individuals to lead in the ministries they're passionate about.

- Gather resources for after-abortion recovery at Focus on the Family (www.focusonthefamily.com), Heartbeat International (www.heartbeatservices.org), or Care Net (www.care-net.org).
- Point people to Support After Abortion (www.support afterabortion.com), where they can find digital support

groups, events, and faith-based or non-faith-based resources for abortion healing.

- Offer support groups for women and men or confidential one-on-one counseling either at your church or off campus for those who may not be ready to admit their past within the church walls.
- Connect with your local college. Sometimes those studying counseling need practicum hours, and they could potentially support women and men who need professional counseling. Or find local Christian counselors who are available, and communicate that resource to your congregation. You can also point people to Christian Care Connect through the American Association of Christian Counselors (https://connect .aacc.net).

In all our personal interactions, whether within or outside church walls, we must remember Romans 2:4: "God's kindness is intended to lead [us] to repentance." It is God who transforms people; we simply need to love on them as He does. God fixes the brokenness, but He partners with us to administer His healing love and grace. It is the Lord alone who transforms hearts and lives.

In the prodigal son parable (see Luke 15), the father does not resent, judge, or shame his lost son or extend a probation period before welcoming him home. Rather, he throws the most lavish, extravagant celebration of joy; that is where we come in. As Amy Ford says, "God invites us to be part of throwing the party."

Let's be the body of Christ, embracing and celebrating life as it is and fostering a thriving environment for life to become what it should be.

Notes

Chapter 1: Pregnancy Resource Centers

1. Mai Bean et al., *Pregnancy Centers Stand the Test of Time: A Legacy of Life and Love Report Series*, Charlotte Lozier Institute, October 13, 2020, 16–18, 44, https://lozierinstitute.org/wp-content/uploads/2020/10/Pregnancy-Center-Report-2020_FINAL.pdf.

2. "Home," Heartbeat International, accessed April 13, 2021, www.heartbeatservices.org/services-home.

3. Bean et al., *Pregnancy Centers Stand the Test of Time*, 16.

4. "About NIFLA," National Institute of Family and Life Advocates, accessed January 20, 2021, https://nifla.org/about-nifla.

5. "Medical Clinical Conversion," National Institute of Family and Life Advocates, accessed January 20, 2021, https://nifla.org/medical-clinic-conversion.

6. "Pro-Life Pregnancy Centers Served 2 Million People, Saved Communities $161M in 2017," Charlotte Lozier Institute, September 5, 2018, https://lozierinstitute.org/pro-life-pregnancy-centers-served-2-million-people-saved-communities-161m-in-2017.

Chapter 2: Not Just Pro-Birth but Pro-Abundant Life

1. Lawrence B. Finer et al., "Reasons U.S. Women Have Abortions: Quantitative and Qualitative Perspectives," *Perspectives on Sexual and Reproductive Health* 37, no. 3 (September 2005): 112, www.guttmacher.org/journals/psrh/2005/reasons-us-women-have-abortions-quantitative-and-qualitative-perspectives.

2. "Induced Abortion in the United States," Guttmacher Institute, September 2019, www.guttmacher.org/fact-sheet/induced-abortion-united-states.

3. Reed Jordan, "Poverty's Toll on Mental Health," *Urban Wire* (blog), Urban Institute, November 25, 2013, www.urban.org/urban-wire/povertys-toll-mental-health.

4. *Schindler's List*, directed by Steven Spielberg (Universal City, CA: Universal Pictures, 1993).

5. "Epilogue," *Les Misérables: Original Motion Picture Soundtrack*, Claude-Michel Schönberg comp., Republic Records, 2013.

Chapter 3: The Importance of Housing

1. Devan M. Crawford et al., "Pregnancy and Mental Health of Young Homeless Women," *American Journal of Orthopsychiatry* 81, no. 2 (April 2011): 173–83, www.ncbi.nlm.nih.gov/pmc/articles/PMC3383651.

2. "Pregnant and Parenting Youth," Covenant House, accessed January 21, 2021, www.covenanthouse.org/pregnant-and-parenting-youth.

3. Crawford et al., "Pregnancy and Mental Health of Young Homeless Women."

4. National Maternity Housing Coalition brochure, accessed August 7, 2020, https://natlhousingcoalition.org/images/NMHC-Brochure.pdf.

5. Mary Peterson, "A Home for the Housing Coalition," Heartbeat International, accessed January 21, 2021, www.heartbeatinternational.org/stay-connected/national -maternity-housing-coalition.

6. "Safe Families: An Alternative to Foster Care," Safe Families for Children, September 8, 2015, https://safe-families.org/blog/2015/alternative-to-foster-care; Kris Faasse, "What If We Could Reach Families before the Crisis? There Would Be Fewer Kids in Foster Care," The Imprint: Youth and Family News, May 21, 2019, https://imprintnews.org /family/what-if-we-could-reach-families-before-the-crisis-there-would-be-fewer-kids-in -foster-care/35037.

Chapter 4: External Pressure

1. Priscilla K. Coleman et al., "Women Who Suffered Emotionally from Abortion: A Qualitative Synthesis of Their Experiences," *Journal of American Physicians and Surgeons* 22, no. 4 (Winter 2017): 113–18, www.jpands.org/vol22no4/coleman.pdf.

2. Jonathan Abbamonte, "Many American Women Have Felt Pressured into Abortions, Study Finds," Population Research Institute, January 24, 2018, www.pop.org/many -american-women-felt-pressured-abortions-study-finds.

3. Susan Dammann, "Forced Abortion in America," Heartbeat International, April 2014, www.heartbeatinternational.org/forced-abortions-in-america.

4. "Down Syndrome and Abortion the Facts," Life Institute, accessed January 21, 2021, https://thelifeinstitute.net/info/down-syndrome-and-abortion-the-facts.

5. Julian Quinones and Arijeta Lajka, "'What kind of society do you want to live in?': Inside the country where Down syndrome is disappearing," CBS News, August 14, 2017, www.cbsnews.com/news/down-syndrome-iceland.

6. Jaime L. Natoli et al., "Prenatal Diagnosis of Down Syndrome: A Systematic Review of Termination Rates (1995–2011)," *Prenatal Diagnosis* 32, no. 2 (February 2012): 142–53, https://pubmed.ncbi.nlm.nih.gov/22418958.

7. "CHD Facts and Stats," Project Heart, accessed January 21, 2021, https://projectheart .org/about-chd/chd-facts-and-stats.

8. Lawrence B. Finer et al., "Reasons U.S. Women Have Abortions: Quantitative and Qualitative Perspectives," *Perspectives on Sexual and Reproductive Health* 37, no. 3 (September 2005): 112, www.guttmacher.org/journals/psrh/2005/reasons-us -women-have-abortions-quantitative-and-qualitative-perspectives.

9. Jan Pavlicek et al., "Parents' Request for Termination of Pregnancy Due to a Congenital Heart Defect of the Fetus in a Country with Liberal Interruption Laws," *Journal of Maternal-Fetal & Neonatal Medicine* 33, no. 17 (January 15, 2019): 2918–26, https://doi .org/10.1080/14767058.2018.1564029.

10. "Data and Statistics on Congenital Heart Defects," Centers for Disease Control and Prevention, December 9, 2020, www.cdc.gov/ncbddd/heartdefects/data.html.

11. "CHD Facts and Stats," Project Heart.

12. *Study of Women Who Have Had an Abortion and Their Views on Church*, Care Net, July 2016, https://cdn2.hubspot.net/hubfs/367552/Downloads/CareNet-research _abortion-in-church.pdf.

13. Finer et al., "Reasons U.S. Women Have Abortions," 112.

14. "Dear Parent Letter," Justice Foundation, accessed January 21, 2021, https: //thejusticefoundation.org/wp-content/uploads/2018/09/Dear-Parent-Letter-Final.pdf.

15. "Life Dynamics Fax to Abortion Clinic," Justice Foundation, accessed January 21, 2021, https://thejusticefoundation.org/wp-content/uploads/2018/09/Life-Dynamics -Fax-to-Abortion-Clinic.pdf.

Chapter 5: Domestic Abuse

1. "Learn More," National Coalition Against Domestic Violence, accessed January 21, 2021, https://ncadv.org/learn-more.

2. "Statistics," National Coalition Against Domestic Violence, accessed January 21, 2021, https://ncadv.org/statistics.

3. Ann M. Moore, Lori Frohwirth, and Elizabeth Miller, "Male reproductive control of women who have experienced intimate partner violence in the United States," *Social Science & Medicine* 70, no. 11 (June 2010): 1737–44, https://doi.org/10.1016/j.socscimed .2010.02.009.

4. "Power and Control: Break Free from Abuse," National Domestic Violence Hotline, accessed January 21, 2021, www.thehotline.org/identify-abuse/power-and-control.

5. Neha A. Deshpande and Annie Lewis-O'Connor, "Screening for Intimate Partner Violence during Pregnancy," *Reviews in Obstetrics and Gynecology* 6, no. 3–4 (2013): 142, www.ncbi.nlm.nih.gov/pmc/articles/PMC4002190.

6. Lawrence B. Finer et al., "Reasons U.S. Women Have Abortions: Quantitative and Qualitative Perspectives," *Perspectives on Sexual and Reproductive Health* 37, no. 3 (September 2005): 113, www.guttmacher.org/journals/psrh/2005/reasons-us -women-have-abortions-quantitative-and-qualitative-perspectives.

7. "Reproductive and Sexual Coercion," American College of Obstetricians and Gynecologists, committee opinion, no. 554 (February 2013), www.acog.org/clinical /clinical-guidance/committee-opinion/articles/2013/02/reproductive-and-sexual -coercion.

8. Jay G. Silverman and Anita Raj, "Intimate Partner Violence and Reproductive Coercion: Global Barriers to Women's Reproductive Control," *PLOS Medicine* 11, no. 9 (September 16, 2014): 2, https://doi.org/10.1371/journal.pmed.1001723.

9. "Reproductive and Sexual Coercion," American College of Obstetricians and Gynecologists.

10. Maeve E. Wallace et al., "Homicide during Pregnancy and the Postpartum Period in Louisiana, 2016–2017," *JAMA Pediatrics* 174, no. 4 (2020): 387–88, https://doi.org /10.1001/jamapediatrics.2019.5853.

11. "Create a Safety Plan: Start Your Path to a Safer Place," National Domestic Violence Hotline, accessed January 22, 2021, www.thehotline.org/create-a-safety-plan.

12. "Preparing to Leave," National Domestic Violence Hotline, accessed January 22, www.thehotline.org/resources/preparing-to-leave-2.

Chapter 6: Sexual Violence and Rape

1. "Understanding Pregnancy Resulting from Rape in the United States," Centers for Disease Control and Prevention, June 1, 2020, www.cdc.gov/violenceprevention /datasources/nisvs/understanding-RRP-inUS.html.

2. "Victims of Sexual Violence: Statistics," RAINN, accessed January 22, 2021, www.rainn.org/statistics/victims-sexual-violence.

3. Melisa M. Holmes et al., "Rape-Related Pregnancy: Estimates and Descriptive Characteristics from a National Sample of Women," *American Journal of Obstetrics and Gynecology* 175, no. 2 (August 1996): 320–25, https://doi.org/10.1016/ s0002-9378(96)70141-2.

4. "Abortion Doesn't Help Rape Victims, Say Women Who've Been There," Elliot Institute, accessed January 22, 2021, https://afterabortion.org/abortion-doesnt-help -rape-victims-say-women-whove-been-there.

5. Lawrence B. Finer et al., "Reasons U.S. Women Have Abortions: Quantitative and Qualitative Perspectives," *Perspectives on Sexual and Reproductive Health* 37, no. 3 (September 2005): 113, www.guttmacher.org/journals/psrh/2005/reasons-us -women-have-abortions-quantitative-and-qualitative-perspectives.

6. "Jennifer Christie," Unbroken: Life beyond Rape, accessed April 17, 2021, https:// unbrokenireland.org/stories/jen-christie.

7. "Tips for Talking with Survivors of Sexual Assault," RAINN, accessed January 22, 2021, www.rainn.org/articles/tips-talking-survivors-sexual-assault.

Chapter 7: Healthy Sexuality

1. "Key Statistics from the National Survey of Family Growth—S Listing," Centers for Disease Control and Prevention, August 14, 2017, www.cdc.gov/nchs/nsfg/key_statistics /s.htm.

2. "Unmarried and Single Americans Week: Sept. 17–23, 2017," *Profile America Facts for Features: CB17-FF.16*, United States Census Bureau, revised August 16, 2017, www .census.gov/content/dam/Census/newsroom/facts-for-features/2017/cb17-ff16.pdf.

3. "Historical Marital Status Tables," United States Census Bureau, December 2020, www.census.gov/data/tables/time-series/demo/families/marital.html.

4. Lauren F. Winner, *Real Sex: The Naked Truth about Chastity* (Grand Rapids, MI: Brazos, 2005), 30.

5. Winner, *Real Sex*, 16–17.

6. Alasdair MacIntyre, *After Virtue: A Study in Moral Theory*, 3rd ed. (Notre Dame, IN: University of Notre Dame Press, 2007), 216.

7. Winner, *Real Sex*, 37.

8. "Key Statistics," Centers for Disease Control and Prevention.

9. "Sexual Behavior, Sexual Attraction, and Sexual Identity in the United States: Data from the 2006–2008 National Survey of Family Growth," *National Health Statistics Reports*, no. 36 (March 3, 2011): 19–20, www.cdc.gov/nchs/data/nhsr/nhsr036.pdf.

10. "Most Unmarried Evangelical Millennials Have Never Had Sex," National Association of Evangelicals, November 29, 2012, www.nae.net/most-unmarried-evangelical-millennials-have-never-had-sex.

11. "Sexually Transmitted Disease Surveillance 2019," Centers for Disease Control and Prevention, April 2021, www.cdc.gov/std/statistics/2019/default.htm.

Chapter 8: Supportive Fathers

1. *Girls*, season 4, episode 6, "Close Up," directed by Richard Shepard, written by Murray Miller, featuring Lena Dunham, Allison Williams, and Jemima Kirke, aired February 22, 2015, on HBO, www.amazon.com/Iowa/dp/B00V333JGK/ref=sr_1_1?dchild=1&keywords=girls+season+4&qid=1618936798&sr=8-1.

2. Brian T. Nguyen et al., "Supporting Women at the Time of Abortion: A Mixed-Methods Study of Male Partner Experiences and Perspectives," *Perspectives on Sexual and Reproductive Health* 50, no. 2 (June 2018): 75–83, https://doi.org/10.1363/psrh.12059.

3. Planned Parenthood v. Danforth, 428 U.S. 52 (1976), https://supreme.justia.com/cases/federal/us/428/52.

4. *Study of Women Who Have Had an Abortion and Their Views on Church*, Care Net, July 2016, https://cdn2.hubspot.net/hubfs/367552/Downloads/CareNet-research_abortion-in-church.pdf, 10.

5. Gretchen Livingston and Kim Parker, "A Tale of Two Fathers," Pew Research Center, June 15, 2011, www.pewsocialtrends.org/2011/06/15/a-tale-of-two-fathers.

Chapter 9: Abortion Pill Reversal

1. "Morning-After Pill," Mayo Clinic, accessed August 8, 2020, www.mayoclinic.org/tests-procedures/morning-after-pill/about/pac-20394730#:~:text=Plan%20B%20One%2DStep%20is,from%20implanting%20in%20the%20uterus.

2. George Delgado et al., "A Case Series Detailing the Successful Reversal of the Effects of Mifepristone Using Progesterone," *Issues in Law & Medicine* 33, no. 1 (2018): 22, https://issuesinlawandmedicine.com/wp-content/uploads/2019/10/Delgado-Revisions-FINAL-1.pdf.

3. Étienne-Émile Baulieu, "1993: RU 486—A Decade on Today and Tomorrow," *Clinical Applications of Mifepristone (RU 486) and Other Antiprogestins*, ed. Molla. S. Donaldson et al. (Washington, DC: National Academies Press, 1993), www.ncbi.nlm.nih.gov/books/NBK236373.

4. Rachel K. Jones, Elizabeth Witwer, and Jenna Jerman, "Abortion Incidence and Service Availability in the United States, 2017," Guttmacher Institute. September 2019, www.guttmacher.org/report/abortion-incidence-service-availability-us-2017.

5. "Thank You for Supporting a Woman's Right to Know about the Abortion Pill Reversal," Heartbeat International, accessed January 21, 2021, www.heartbeatinternational.org/aprn-pledge-ty.

6. Kim Hayes, "First Doctor to Deliver a Baby Rescued from Abortion Pill Has a Heart for Life," Pregnancy Help News, December 29, 2020, https://pregnancyhelpnews.com /first-doctor-to-deliver-a-baby-rescued-from-abortion-pill-has-a-heart-for-life.

7. "Abortion Pill Reversal Is a Real Option," Real Options, accessed August 11, 2020, www.realoptions.net/abortion-pill-reversal-is-a-real-option.

8. G. Dante, V. Vaccaro, and F. Facchinetti, "Use of Progestagens during Early Pregnancy," *Facts, Views, & Vision in ObGyn* 5, no. 1 (2013): 66–71, www.ncbi.nlm.nih .gov/pmc/articles/PMC3987350.

9. Mitchell D. Creinin et al., "Mifepristone Antagonization with Progesterone to Prevent Medical Abortion," *Obstetrics & Gynecology* 135, no. 1 (January 2020): 158, https://journals.lww.com/greenjournal/Abstract/2020/01000/Mifepristone _Antagonization_With_Progesterone_to.21.aspx.

10. "Blocking Mifepristone Action with Progesterone," ClinicalTrials.gov, January 22, 2020, https://clinicaltrials.gov/ct2/show/NCT03774745?cond=NCT03774745.&draw= 2&rank=1.

11. "Can the Abortion Pill Be Reversed after You Have Taken It?," Planned Parenthood, September 14, 2017, www.plannedparenthood.org/learn/teens/ask-experts/can-the -abortion-pill-be-reversed-after-you-have-taken-it.

12. Delgado et al., "Case Series Detailing the Successful Reversal," 22, 26.

13. "2019 AAPLOG Position Statement on Abortion Pill Reversal," American Association of Pro-Life Obstetricians and Gynecologists, February 2019, https://aaplog.org/wp -content/uploads/2019/02/2019-AAPLOG-Statement-on-Abortion-Pill-Reversal.pdf.

14. "Counseling and Waiting Periods for Abortion," Guttmacher Institute, April 2021, www.guttmacher.org/state-policy/explore/counseling-and-waiting-periods-abortion.

15. "Medication Guide for Mifeprex," US Food and Drug Administration, March 2016, www.accessdata.fda.gov/drugsatfda_docs/label/2019/020687s022lbl.pdf#page=2.

16. "Medication Guide for Mifeprex," US Food and Drug Administration.

17. Delgado et al., "Case Series Detailing the Successful Reversal," 22.

18. "Sharing Abortion Pill Reversal in Your Community," Heartbeat International, accessed May 20, 2020, www.heartbeatinternational.org/our-work/apr/itemlist/tag /abortion%20pill%20reversal.

19. "About," Steno Institute, accessed January 22, 2021, http://stenoinstitute.org/about.

Chapter 10: Healing after Abortion

1. *Study of Women Who Have Had an Abortion and Their Views on Church*, Care Net, July 2016, https://cdn2.hubspot.net/hubfs/367552/Downloads/CareNet-research_abortion -in-church.pdf.

2. *Study of Women Who Have Had an Abortion*, Care Net.

3. *Study of Women Who Have Had an Abortion*, Care Net.

4. Keith Getty, Kristyn Getty, and Stuart Townend, "Compassion Hymn," copyright © 2009 Thankyou Music (PRS) (adm. worldwide at CapitolCMGPublishing.com excluding

Europe which is adm. by Integrity Music, part of the David C Cook family. Songs@
integritymusic.com). All rights reserved. Used by permission.

Chapter 11: Church Participation in the Pro-Life Movement

1. Dennis Quinn, "Few U.S. Sermons Mention Abortion, though Discussion Varies by
Religious Affiliation and Congregation Size," Pew Research Center, April 29, 2020,
www.pewresearch.org/fact-tank/2020/04/29/few-u-s-sermons-mention-abortion-though
-discussion-varies-by-religious-affiliation-and-congregation-size.

2. *Study of Women Who Have Had an Abortion and Their Views on Church*, Care Net, July
2016, https://cdn2.hubspot.net/hubfs/367552/Downloads/CareNet-research_abortion
-in-church.pdf.

3. *Merriam-Webster*, s.v. "compassion (n.)," accessed January 20, 2021, www.merriam
-webster.com/dictionary/compassion.

4. "Home," Heartbeat International, accessed January 20, 2021, www.heartbeatservices
.org/services-home.

5. "Fast Facts about American Religion," Hartford Institute for Religion Research,
accessed August 7, 2020, http://hirr.hartsem.edu/research/fastfacts/fast_facts.html.

6. Tony Evans, quoted in Amy Ford, "Churches: Teamwork Can Save Lives," Focus on the
Family, June 29, 2020, www.focusonthefamily.com/pro-life/churches-teamwork-can
-save-lives.

7. Dietrich Bonhoeffer, *The Cost of Discipleship*, trans. Chr. Kaiser Verlag München (New
York: Touchstone, 1995).

8. Quinn, "Few U.S. Sermons Mention Abortion."

9. Catherine T. Coyle, "Men and Abortion: A Review of Empirical Reports concerning the
Impact of Abortion on Men," *Internet Journal of Mental Health* 3, no. 2 (2006): 2,
https://print.ispub.com/api/0/ispub-article/3683.

10. Catherine T. Coyle and Vincent M. Rue, "A Thematic Analysis of Men's Experience
with a Partner's Elective Abortion," Wiley Online Library, October 1, 2015, https://doi.
org/10.1002/cvj.12010.

About Save the Storks

Save the Storks is a national nonprofit ministry that exists to inspire cultural change by shaping compelling pro-life narratives and empowering strategic partners, like pregnancy resource centers (PRCs), to serve and value every life. They believe that in order to end abortion, people must be educated on its realities, inspired to value life, and equipped to respond in love. Changed actions are a result of changed minds and hearts.

One of their deepest desires is to change the conversation around the pro-life movement. They don't want to engage the current debate; they seek to reimagine it. By shifting the focus away from divisive language to a dialogue of hope and true empowerment, they seek to meet women in their time of need with love, compassion, and action to truly support them.

Save the Storks was founded in 2012 with the goal of seeing abortion become unthinkable in our lifetime. To make abortion unthinkable, it is more vital to change the attitudes and perceptions of individuals than to change laws. Instead of debating terms and definitions, we tell stories of real-life transformation of women and men who previously believed choosing life for their child was not an option.

Aside from engaging in the cultural conversation on the pro-life issue, Save the Storks equips PRCs to reach more abortion-vulnerable individuals. Their work includes building and launching mobile medical units (MMUs). These vehicles are designed with medical-grade equipment and materials and offer free onboard ultrasounds and pregnancy tests to women at their moment of decision. These buses provide the privacy and comfort of a doctor's office on wheels. PRCs own and operate MMUs, taking them into their communities where they're needed most.

Four out of five women who board an MMU and have a positive pregnancy test choose life.*

As Save the Storks grew, they discovered more ways in which to support the lifesaving work of PRCs. Through consulting, training, branding, marketing, fundraising, and more, Save the Storks empowers the pro-life movement to serve women like never before.

Micah 6:8 is the compass:

> He has shown you, O mortal, what is good.
> And what does the LORD require of you?
> To act justly and to love mercy
> and to walk humbly with your God.

---

* Based on stats reported by participating mobile ministry partners.

About the Authors

Natasha Smith

Natasha Smith hails from a small town in northern Michigan and now lives in Colorado Springs, Colorado, where she supports pro-life organizations by telling stories through writing, video, and photography. Her academic background is in communications and biblical theology with a focus on the Old Testament. Her love for the pro-life movement is grounded in the understanding that all life has value because every life is created in the image of God (Gen. 1:27). In her free time, Natasha enjoys dialoguing with others, studying Scripture, and exploring the magnificent mountains of Colorado.

Brittany Smith

Brittany Smith has worked as a journalist and a content strategist in digital marketing. She is now a staff writer for the pro-life organization Save the Storks. She loves telling stories that show how the pro-life movement truly cares about women, that women are stronger than our culture wants them to believe, and that it's always possible to change our own story. Brittany graduated from Grove City College in Grove City, Pennsylvania. She hails from North Carolina and now lives in Colorado Springs, Colorado, where she tries to explore the Rockies whenever she isn't writing.